CHINESE CONTEMPORARY ART SINCE 1989

Somogy éditions d'art
Directeur éditorial : Nicolas Neumann
Responsable éditoriale : Stéphanie Méséguer
Suivi éditorial : Océane Monange
Contribution éditoriale : Stéphanie Cooper-Slockyj
Fabrication : Béatrice Bourgerie et Mélanie Le Gros

www.somogy.fr

978-2-7572-1254-7
Dépôt légal : mai 2018
Imprimé en République tchèque (Union européenne)

Lü Peng

CHINESE CONTEMPORARY ART SINCE 1989

Translated from the Chinese by Bruce Gordon Doar

SOMOGY
ÉDITIONS
D'ART

This work is an outcome of the Art Stories Project (sjzx 2018001) administered by the Contemporary Visual Art Reasearch Center at the Sichuan Fine Arts Institute and funded by the Academic Publishing Fund of the Sichuan Fine Arts Institute.

Foreword

Examining Today's Historical Background

Examining "historical consequences" is not just the task of the historian; everyone concerned about human life, not to mention the fate of individuals, will wittingly or unwittingly evaluate and utilize "historical consequences". From the point of view of history, we are now more than 16 years into the 21st century, only different characters and events from the 20th century are making an impact. Not only that. Given that most of the topics we must consider today come from the 20th century, that many of the facts that emerge derive from historical causes, and that many of the things that have not yet happened but might yet happen are connected with problems of the century that only ended 16 years ago, consequently when we discuss and evaluate today's "contemporary art", how can we flatly and adamantly refuse to mention "yesterday" and simply discuss what is designated as belonging to "today"?

People are in the habit of using the terms "continuity", "discontinuity", or "change" in discussions of historical development, and for people with little creativity – and who are often regarded as conservatives or as people with vested interests – historical "continuity" is of prime importance; yet for radicals and trendies, "uniqueness" and "discontinuities" are vital to mankind's history of development. In fact, all of these either/or views are simply one-sided claims that describe, analyze, and judge historical events that have occurred in a specific context based on a particular position or world view which we are obligated to maintain today as our attitude and methods.

We can certainly say that this 21st century is different from the 20th; for example, 20 years ago in China, when the young Chinese scholar, now Professor Yi Dan, returned from the United States in 1997 and wrote *On the American Information Superhighway*, there were very few people in this country who understood or used Internet technology, yet today in China even small remote village inns generally have Wi-Fi that immediately puts us in contact with any place in the world. In addition to the physical appearance of relative stability – which is already highly relative – great changes have taken place in the world, and if you will, almost everyone is a node that can connect with people anywhere in the world and engage in dialogue with them, resulting in both parties being subject to ever-expanding ripples of change. However, this does not signify a denial of the history of telephone communications; historically speaking, it would be a joke to say that the production of wood facilitated ocean-going ships, because this would make light of both the 17th century scientific revolution in Europe and the industrialization process. In fact, the genes of human thought and ideas derive from the great geographical discoveries of adventurers and merchants, by Newton, by Watt, and of course by Darwin or Einstein; all those inventions benefiting human lives directly and indirectly influenced human civilization.

Indeed, technology has led to the rapid and constant development of transportation and communications, accelerating concentrated and frequent exchanges between human civilizations and cultures, so that exchanges between different countries, regions, and peoples can technically be fully synchronized, with no "time lag". But a problem simultaneously also arises in this situation. Science and technology facilitate circulation and convenience, at the same time as they also shut down and control, so that we can directly observe the following outcome: regardless of so-called global or regional communication modes, people are invariably subject to guidance and interference by different confining sources of power. Even when an event is reported, people in different nations and areas receive information that is not only different, but is differently described, analyzed, and judged.

People who are lazy or have ulterior motives are fond of using the fact that there is always a "positive" or "negative" side to everything or that its application might result in the appearance or existence of problems for which they want to avoid responsibility, but even terms like "artificial intelligence" remind people that the "human gene" in the future world will be completely different from today, nor is there any reason to assume that responsibility will be optional. Freud long ago reminded us that consciousness is the tip of the iceberg of the "unconscious" and that humans have limitless potential, but it is difficult to defend the idea of psychological automatism.

Indeed, we cannot simply use the year 2000 as the line of demarcation separating the 20th century from the 21st century; this attitude certainly also reminds us that we also explain the 20th century in terms of the last decades of the 19th century, when unbridled colonial expansion led Western powers to establish absolute domination over the world and set the initial scene for globalization. If, for example, we were to look for the earlier factors in the rise of mass leisure culture, then we need to go back to the Industrial Revolution. Simply put, the main features of the early 20th century had already emerged much earlier.

In the 19th century in China's coastal areas, paintings influenced by Western art (mainly European art) could easily be seen. Western merchants living in China hoped, of course, that Western culture could be part of their daily lives, and it is not difficult to understand why the Western-style watercolors, oil paintings, and drawings common in the 18th century became widely popular in the 19th century in the coastal cities of Guangdong. Can this phenomenon be a "semi-colonial" synthesis? Does the fact that George Chinnery was teaching painting in Guangzhou and that Guan Qiaochang (Lam Qua) and others were his students a de facto result of colonialism?

> My friends are becoming numerous among the Chinese. I am recognized wherever I go. I do not feel the confinement at Canton so much as I should but for my acquaintance and intercourse with the people. All classes live at the hospital – male and female, young and old, from the infant of a month to the gray head of eighty years, rich and poor, officers of government and their subjects. Nothing but kindness from Europeans of whatever nationality – Scotch, English, French, or German. There are two promising youths now with a knowledge of English, wishing to become doctors themselves. Some others have applied for situations at the hospital. One of the lads is a brother of Lam Qua, a painter, a pupil of George Chinnery, Esq. He is a great lover of the medical profession, and regrets that he is too old to become a doctor himself.[1]

The above text is from a letter written by the American missionary and physician Dr Peter Parker (1804-1888) in 1837 to his American friends. This pious missionary took 144 days to travel by boat from New York and arrived in Guangzhou in late October 1834, where he soon established a private clinic. It is immediately apparent that Lam Qua developed his own language of painting. However, when we look through this period of art history in Europe, we note that: in the United Kingdom, Turner had effectively painted in 1842 what is said to be one of the earliest works of impressionism, *Snowstorm: Steamship off a Harbour's Mouth*; the pre-Raphaelite painters were beginning to use photography; Gustave Courbet painted his "expressive realist" work titled *Burial at Ornans* in 1850; Edouard Manet had begun painting *Olympia* which he would complete in 1863; and Claude Monet painted *Impression: Sunrise* in 1872. In fact, in 1893, well after the First and Second Opium Wars and their aftermath, Chinese society was heading for total collapse, and in 1900, the Boxer Rebellion left the Qing dynasty with a tenuous grip on government. At this time, accompanying the Industrial Revolution in Europe, new artists such as Seurat, Van Gogh, Gauguin, and Cezanne were widely known throughout Europe, and the style and language of these artists not only promoted modernism throughout Europe and the United States, but by the 1920s, 1930s, and 1940s they also influenced Chinese artists.

The Second World War led to changes in the political, economic, and cultural spheres of different countries in different directions, and the accompanying development of science and technology led to complex interaction constituting a new phase of globalization. Even though the Cold War split the world into two camps, a lot of the literature shows that the process of globalization exerted an irresistible influence on the "civilization" purists, and the results of the Industrial Revolution and the rise of colonial culture ultimately led to the end of the unitary development of civilization. The Cold War seemed to be a rehearsal of a human drama, a dramatic process featuring formation, climax, and denouement. The end of the Cold War filled most Western politicians with a sense of victory, because the opposing party lost the battle and completely fell apart, something understood to be "the end of history". We know that the end of history was, of course, not a fact, given that history survives together with humanity. Westerners subsequently saw that racial and religious hatred and terrorism were no less threatening than the Soviet bloc. On the one hand, in the 20th century and the early 21st century, traffic, communications and computer technology have accelerated contacts around the world, while satellite TV has resulted in the possibility of any national program being broadcast globally; unless one country's management system is restricted, the degree, speed, and scale of openness are something the people enjoying the telegraph, steamboat, and railway in the early 20th century could only imagine in their wildest dreams. Indeed, since 1978 not only Russia but even China have strengthened the further liberalization of international trade and, with the development of the commodity economy, elements of capitalism can be seen everywhere and globalized links are all the more apparent. On the other hand, the global flows of labor, capital, and resources caused by globalization seriously affect the relative stability of countries and regions; it is difficult to say that protests against globalization in Seattle or any European city have no basis in reality. Yet capital has no particular fondness for history and as long as there is a profit potential it will be desperate to take up the challenge. For example, in the art field the changes are obvious, and at the same time as increasingly lively art expositions have been promoting art sales since the 1990s, the rapidity of this development has blurred the boundaries between art historians, critics, art consultants, curators, brokers, and teachers, and if the possibility exists, a person regarded as a serious art historian can be a consultant for an art expo specifically designed to sell art, and the head of an advertising company can in turn become an art curator.

In fact, capital reduces the political barriers built on ideology, and it is only because different countries have different political structures that capital is able to be different in nature and play different roles in different regions: if a European collector (who is certainly also an investor in art) chooses new art from China or Asia according to his or her own values, after he invests money (capital) in Asian contemporary art and the market yields an incredibly high profit, at the same time as he makes a profit he is also guiding values. Yet a national art organization with an entrenched ideological position will possibly only waste taxpayers' money on government programs with no market results, as the difficulties of investing and achieving a return on investment in the world of globalized culture and values demonstrate. The reasons for this complexity come, of course, from values and positions, but between different countries and different institutions with different cultural backgrounds, as well as between different targeted interests among those involved in cooperation, there will always appear disagreements and contradictions that are not simply a part of marketization. This is somewhat like the situation with a KFC outlet operating in a Chinese city and using inferior ingredients to swindle consumers: you do not know which link in the process is problematic – employee training, cultural habits, the management system, or implementation monitoring. There is no doubt that when viewers around the world sit in front of their television sets to watch the annual Academy Awards broadcast, it is the same American program everywhere.

Obviously, the tide of globalization does not mean that we all must have an inclusive perspective, as for example in this following introduction by Thomas Piketty to his ideas as published in China's *Reference News*:

> First of all, I regret that this book contains little about China, India, and other emerging nations, even though this book begins with a discussion of the pattern of global GDP distribution and the rise of emerging powers such as China and India. I wanted to be able to have a global vision, by including emerging economies, but data on emerging countries did not attain a desirable level, mainly

> due to a lack of historical data. I wanted my book to be able to trace back one or two centuries, but the Chinese do not have data available for reference. China only began to have relevant data in the 1980s, and China's taxation data are incomplete. For research, income tax and property registration are declared by individuals, and so the data have serious limitations. In China especially, the top income bracket is often not very good at reporting, and tax information is incomplete; incomplete reporting on property and property taxation is a big problem in China. I do not even know if China has property and inheritance taxes, and at least for now we have no material and data.[2]

In 2014, the French economist Thomas Piketty (b. 1971) who authored the best selling *Capital in the Twenty-First Century* (2013) made the above comments when asked about emerging nations and in particular about solutions to the problem of inequality of wealth in China. Piketty is, of course, discussing the field of economic income and wealth distribution, which has nothing to do with the art which I wish to discuss, but this young scholar's methodology follows an approach similar to how we observe questions of art: history and the questions we confront are not questions to which we can apply theoretical or speculative analysis.

At the same time, Piketty not only mentions how the lack of sufficient relevant data for China constitutes an obstacle to economic research, but he expresses the reality clearly and we can perceive links to other spheres in China: Is there a civilizational reason for history without data? What was the political background that explains why it was only in the 1980s that China began to produce data? Did the absence of "individual declarations" imply a moral failing and a systemic problem? What are the possibilities and actual status of taxes such as those on property and inheritance in China? Speaking from an economic perspective, Piketty could perhaps intuitively provide a solution that China could reference, as for example that "China needs to develop progressive income and property taxes to limit the phenomenon of wealth inequality, and restrict the accumulation of wealth", but from the outset he seems to doubt such a proposal because he makes it clear: "I regret to see that income and property of distribution in China is still not transparent". Here, he touches on a key question encountered in examining different fields in China: Why are things this way? Even if "the historical experience of France, the United Kingdom, and Germany is useful for China", the basic premise of these experiences – the political system – is completely different from that of China, and as a consequence the civilizational backgrounds of Europe and China are also quite divergent. In such a situation, even if China and all other countries are enmeshed in "globalization",

China was destined to have its own particularity. In the first decade of the new century, in China's art market serious problems were continually emerging – excessive speculation, illegal fund-raising, instances of forgery, and excessive artistic property transactions in the name of so-called "art financing"; these phenomena cannot be passed off simply as results arising from the trend of following Western capitalist market logic. China has a special civilizational background, and for almost a century it has been embroiled in a dilemma in its political system and social problems, with the result that at almost any period or stage people have been conflicted by interwoven and internal political, economic, and art problems that deprive those concerned with the ontology of art of the right to speak, so that people increasingly less regard art as a pure spiritual home. At the same time, there is global discussion about China's economy: why is China's contemporary art also discussed everywhere, even if when some critics gather one hardly hears any discussion about "art"? Broadly speaking, apart from using the word "art", art circles do not seem able to provide any simple classifications, ideas, or values.

The uninterrupted, interactive flow of information would seem to hint at the need for the establishment of a global system but, from the ongoing activities and bickering of the United Nations, no global system yet exists, so when people are assessing a significant event in a particular country or city, there is a lack of consistency and no judgment can be made. For example, on 13 April 2016, the *Financial Times* reported that when Jack Ma acquired the *South China Morning Post*, Western and Chinese reports of this were totally different; Tom Mitchell wrote, under the headline that "Ma cannot win as owner of the *South China Morning Post*", because as he explained, "some people will always suspect him of doing Beijing's bidding." In fact, even in the economic field where there are only business facts, there is no business ontology, so there are no shared and constant rules. As for art, it began its lone journey in the late 19th century; though this was relative, even in the 21th century with its information cloud processing, an art standard is even more lacking. This is not to say that a cleaner in an art gallery can throw out an art installation, but that the concepts proposed by a general curator at any international biennale will have no influence, and apart from commercial need, words such as "authoritative", "famous", or "internationally well-known" have no meaning. "Contemporary" does not have its own Baudelaire, Oscar Wilde, or Ruskin. Clement Greenberg's or Arthur Danto's art ideas and vocabulary are irrelevant in the Chinese context.

To a certain extent, global warming and environmental issues transcend traditional ideological disputes, mainly because the rapid deterioration of the ecological environment is fundamentally disastrous for humankind. Periodic meetings of the Intergovernmental Panel on Climate Change indicate the degree of urgency required in solving environmental problems, but when it comes to the specific responsibilities and obligations of different states, proceedings are marked by evasion and disputes. Thus, an increase in national and religious conflicts, the ongoing and persistent ideological disputes, the constant vicious global terrorism[3], and the general environmental crisis further burden the planet, when environmental problems are the greatest challenge humans face in the 21st century. Yet, the evolution and basic complexity of proposals to deal with this problem are disproportionate, which seems to say: the solution to any problem faced by all humans requires a consistent attitude if it is to be truly implemented – just like the Second World War. The entire world is locked in discussion of questions concerning survival and development, but high-level development of the economy has prompted a process of urbanization, ushering in new urban problems; revolutions and political movements that lead to deaths are on the decrease and are being replaced by new regional wars and religious conflicts; nuclear weapons designed to maintain national security have intensified world tensions; and although the advancement of science and technology by leaps and bounds has brought us improved nutrition, living conditions, and new tools of innovation, it has also provided more convenient technology for tyranny and terrorism. As a result, on the basis of civilization and traditions, differences between political systems, special interests, and natural conditions, concepts and labels used in the process of human communication and exchange remain colourful, and it remains difficult to reach a decisive consensus; at the same time, on the basis of the reality of models of globalization and regionalization, it is difficult to apply terminology relating to progress to the world. Even the nature of "democracy" has been given multiple and even bizarre explanations.

Furthermore, when we overlook long-standing historical issues that are related to a country's stability, we see that in view of the many gaps between the world's nations, created by long histories and cultural backgrounds, deep-seated national psychologies, and durable and stable interests, that must be bridged, these determine the criteria for "globalization" that different countries extend to contemporary culture. In the art world, when artists are only involved with questions that directly and indirectly confront them, it is possible for them to express their views and opinions and propose their own specific solutions. When determining what the main issue is in a world plagued with financial crisis, political recession, widespread war and terrorism, issues of art and culture are largely undermined; a living artist must emphasize his or her true inner voice, and from the perspective of art history, mankind's artistic spirit must remain sensitive to the grand narrative and to microcosmic feelings. Indeed, it is in the process of each individual's perception of the world and expressions of opinion that we are able to find the code of history: this is the price we must pay for the basic elements of human existence.

When the depression in the spirit of the arts and humanities stemming from the crushing of values and the hollowing out of forms by globalization result in the loss of positions of value and the blurring of standards, art becomes at most an ordinary psychological narrative or a pathological performance, and the ideas and concepts that provide universal human solace can scarcely make any contribution to history: this is the problem we face.

In any case, globalization heightens the possibility of further uncertainty and openness. Even if people are in a dilemma concerning the world's future, there will never again be a single center of political and cultural power, the Internet must result in the concept of democracy being generally implemented, and any node at any time may become a focus of world concern or disappear without a trace or shadow. The disappearance of regulation will also provide humans with a vast creative space, and a stability of values might result in change because of different backgrounds in civilizations, like the tide of refugees ushered in by the war in Syria; in this case, thinking about different solutions is a direction in which people must strive.[4]

In short, historical differences and new integrations, continuities, and ruptures, forced and natural change, globalization and regionalism, collapse and growth, change and integration, and so on, all these intellectual and intelligent movements will help us understand the code of human history, and the supply of creativity will address the corresponding scarcity (depression) in humanity and society, and maintain the vigor and vitality of the human race.

Pessimism's primary function hints at the problem, which is that humans need idealism. We could probably return to a golden age, or have a future we could look forward to, if we could locate and reconstruct the code of history. That code is the blueprint for an ideal society; for this troubled world it has been Confucius's construction of a social order, Plato's ideal State, or a return to Rome, the Han and Tang dynasties or the glory of Florence; regardless of the form in which it evolves, from birth to the grave, from the concept to the symbol of the spiritual order, everything would be fully integrated. Even if we cannot adequately use language to reach its essence, we can glimpse it through the clues provided by history and the present. After all, we do not need Wittgenstein to explain it to us and we must remain silent about things we cannot speak of, because the history of the spirit has purpose and silence will not prejudice its greatness.

Notes

1. The author has taken this from the Chinese translation of Edward V. Gulick, Peter Parker and the Opening of China, Cambridge Massachusetts: Harvard University Press, 1973, titled Bojia yu Zhongguo de Kaifang (Guangxi Normal University Press, 2008, p. 262). However, the original English edition does not quote Peter Parker's letter of mid-1837, and the translator has taken the text from Rev. George B. Stevens, The Life, Letters, and Journals of the Rev. and Hon. Peter Parker: Missionary, Physician and Diplomatist, the Father of Medical Missions and Founder of the Opthalmic Hospital in Canton, Boston and Chicago: Congregational Sunday-School and Publishing Society, preface dated 1896.

2. "Yong Zhengshui Jiejue Zhongguo Caifu Bu Pingdeng" (Use Taxes to Solve China's Wealth Inequalities) (in Chinese), Cankao Xiaoxi (*Reference News*), 12 June 2014, p. 11.

3. In the global context, the nationalism behind the clash of civilizations – even though many intellectuals point out that there is no connection between terrorism and civilizations – came to the fore again with the attack on the offices of Charlie Hebdo on 7 January 2015. People recalled the history of the Crusades, and when looking for the layered causes of this event, people again asked how different nationalities

and religions could live together in peace. Are not poverty and inequality vis-à-vis Western arrogance and prejudice still causes of a clash between civilizations? The tragedy that occurred in Paris in November 2015 is simply the critical problem that many countries around the world now face.

4. As an example, although the wave of refugees provides Europe with a security-related dilemma, humanity has never had rules stating which nationalities could only live in fixed places, and people have the natural and historical right to freely move about. At the same time, more opposition to receiving refugees is coming from the nations of Eastern Europe and they seem to have forgotten how during the Nazi period other nations accepted them.

The Failure of Ideological Excitement

"Ideological excitement" is a term I coined to encapsulate the mentality of Chinese modernism between 1979 and June 1989: aggressive and revelatory until the shots were fired. On 5 February 1989, the *Exhibition of Chinese Contemporary Art* was closed because of the shot fired by Xiao Lu, and at a noisy gathering in a classroom at the Central Academy of Fine Arts a youth in a green bandanna brandished a sword (made of wood) at the artist Xu Bing, as he phrased a long-winded question that people could not hear clearly. Chaos prevailed then, and when the exhibition was closed again a few days later, there was a return to chaos, tension and confusion. One of the curators of the exhibition, Gao Minglu, was anxious to deal with all these incidents and problems one by one. Later, he concluded:

> Now this exhibition, in confronting society and the art scene, has not only been pervaded by a sense of tragedy but has perpetuated a "hooligan consciousness", social decline from heroism and a tragic sense of life. Like the Chinese bacchanalian spirit depicted in the movie *Red Sorghum*, there was a lot of bravado, because the life experiences of individuals were not grounded in a rigorous rationality and a natural healthy state but were related to primitivism and the worship of sex. The brush can instinctively

> be used to touch on any subject but this cannot equate with "genital art", and the genitals can't be used to paint; the desires of art and life are, after all, not one and the same and there must be some sublimation.[1]

In the *Exhibition*, the artists Gao Xian, Gao Qiang, and Li Qun represented male genitalia with enormous inflated balloons in their work entitled *Midnight Mass: The Final Trial of the Century*, and the "sexuality" of this work created an uproar. Even though the artists wanted to use the work to give "sexuality" "new aesthetic significance" as a basic truth by highlighting D. H. Lawrence's view that sex is the "key to life and spiritual regeneration", Gao Minglu was filled with revulsion by these simulated genitals. Fan Di'an, another curator of the exhibition, recalled that when the Chinese and English names for the Exhibition were being discussed, some painters, in the spirit of the times, were unhappy with the term "modern" and wanted something more "avant-garde". He said that "this touched on two problems: the understanding and evaluation of avant-garde art within the art world and what society could tolerate". The latter revealed the psychological climate of the society at the time, given that there was no diminution in the avant-garde art world's desire to "charge" ahead.

Li Xianting's attitude was completely different from that of Gao Minglu and others. When he heard that Xiao Lu had fired a gun at her installation work, he described how he felt excited and stimulated; the gunshot expressed his own excitement, "releasing hopes that had long been suppressed", as he described it. Gao Minglu had been dismayed and angered by the abrupt firing of the gun; for him this was not simply because this "performance" had neither been scheduled nor had it been approved, but because it seemed to him to be an act that belonged to a reality beyond academic logic and an indulgence in non-conscious and irrational non-culture. Even many years later, he regarded the abstruse concept of "spiritual totality" as characteristic of contemporary art. Li Xianting's feeling most conformed to the social context: before and after 1988, the rapid development of the commodity economy had changed the face of social life, the structure of the planned economy was being subverted, a population for whom work had become destabilized was moving about the country, and many artists from remote areas were coming to Beijing to seek opportunities, thereby becoming part of the increasingly large army of "jobless" drifters. Around 1989, the concept of the Yuanmingyuan artists' village became widely known in the art world. In fact, the number of free artists continued to grow, and there was a break from the lifestyles of the past; the "units" of the planned economy began to lose their significance for young artists, there was a radical break with previous lifestyles, and a clear and specific rebellion was taking shape.

An open revolt in the field of art began after 1978; when Gao Xiaohua and Cheng Conglin, students of the Sichuan Academy of Fine Arts, completed their Scar Art works, doubts concerning earlier history were ignited. Gao Xiaohua's *Why* (1978) clearly questioned the Cultural Revolution: Why did hatred break out within the ranks of students? What was the revolution they wanted to defend? How could universal truths be demonstrated? The figures in this painting were oppressed by their grey and gloomy environment; the work depicted a time without hope, a time that provided no reason for enduring, and a time for which no legitimacy could be found. The questions posed by *Why* were unavoidable, and they were in sharp contrast to the attitudes and even the ideological positions created by the themes, styles, and expression in the treatment of all topics in earlier Cultural Revolution art. Cheng Conglin's *Snow on an Unrecorded Day in 1968* (1979) used dramatic conflict in the manner of Surikov to pose a political question: What in the end was the political nature of the tragic and cruel "armed conflict" during the Cultural Revolution? Since the political nature of the Cultural Revolution itself had lost its legitimacy, did the proletarian revolution that provided the justification for the "armed conflict" continue to have legitimacy? Soon, because the face of the peasant in Luo Zhongli's *Father* was held to be lacking in vitality, this work too came in for criticism from critics driven by established ideology: perhaps this bitter and possibly illiterate old peasant symbolized or stood for all Chinese fathers! Regardless of the specific reasons, the works submitted by these students of the Sichuan Academy of Fine Arts in fact constituted a critique of history; even though official artistic standards had not been revoked, those who had experienced the Cultural Revolution were more willing to affirm such new art, rather than negate it. There was a legitimating basis for this: Since the Cultural Revolution was an "error" as a political movement, art that questioned and criticized the Cultural Revolution was legitimate. Very few people could apply long-standing official artistic criteria to assess the new art that was appearing, and at almost the same time impressionist and expressionist art was coming onto the scene, making it possible for what had been regarded as bourgeois humanism to be recognized. This is why He Duoling's sentimental and complex humane works could so readily assume an acknowledged place in the art world at the same time as impressionist and expressionist paintings by Zhou Chunya and Zhang Xiaogang. It can be seen that the targets of critique started with the theme and then went on to look at the specific expression of that theme, completely disregarding the aesthetic criteria championed in Cultural Revolution art ("red, light, bright"; "tall, large, and total"). Because the Cultural Revolution had just ended, memories of tragic experiences were still fresh. People were little concerned with thinking about art methods and questions of style; the story and its political stance and attitude sufficed to allow audiences to temporarily ignore art questions. For most of the audience, art issues removed from their original knowledge of the background of the work (their visual experience of realistic painting) did not exist; they basically had no visual experience, having never seen modernist art.

Intellectuals concerned with politics define the political background between 1978 and 1983 as representing the purge of a clique within the Party. After the arrest in 1976 of the Gang of Four clique comprising Jiang Qing, Yao Wenyuan, Zhang Chunqiao, and Wang Hongwen by an older generation of Communists, power in the Party was in the hands of victims of political persecution during the Cultural Revolution. However, in the decade following the Cultural Revolution in 1966 the Gang of Four won political power in every city in the country, and so it became very important to eliminate these forces, and provide political legitimacy for their elimination. At the same time, the power structure required a period of consolidation and it was especially important to have as wide a range of support as possible, and this was why the feelings of deep resentment occasioned by the Cultural Revolution were so widely utilized. Scar Art was of course a response to such a political background, and there was a major reason why the Scar Art that emerged in Chongqing won the support of the China Artists Association: important officials in the art world such as Jiang Feng and Wang Zhaowen were so persecuted in political movements and the Cultural Revolution that after they were restored to positions of status within official art institutions, it was natural for them to use Scar Art to eliminate and critique the political effects of the Cultural Revolution. Scar Art was regarded as being of great importance and was supported by official art organizations; the Chinese Artists' Association and the Sichuan Academy of Fine Arts staged a special exhibition and seminar of the art of these young people in Beijing.

The political fate of the Beijing Stars art group was not as smooth as that of the students who produced Scar Art; from the beginning the Stars artists had more freedom to choose a public venue for their own exhibition, though they did not qualify as a legitimate exhibition. Their show was cancelled the moment it opened, which led to the Stars adopting a more radical course of action: they staged a street demonstration in the hope of having their exhibition reinstated. In China at this time, the real instability was not a parade of young people, but the remnant forces of the Gang of Four, and the Stars' use of the slogan of "democracy" to criticize the Gang of Four made it politically difficult for the government to shut down their demonstration. The personal experience of one of the leaders of the Beijing Artists' Association, Liu Xun, revealed the vicissitudes of his political career,[2] and in 1978 he petitioned Hu Yaobang and finally recovered the rights he lost in the anti-rightist campaign of the Communist Party. During his tenure as Deputy President of the Beijing Artists' Association, his support of the Stars accorded with the political climate, and the support provided by Jiang Feng as head of the China Artists' Association showed that the political line at this time was quite clear: The Gang of Four clique and its followers were in political battle with the older generation of leaders of the Communist Party and their sympathizers. For Deng Xiaoping, who had just acquired political power, winning support of the majority was his most important political policy. Therefore, the Stars were also finally able to organize their own exhibition at the National Art Museum of China, and in contrast could openly display their works on the fences outside the gallery.

The movement to "eliminate spiritual pollution" that began in 1983 was like a familiar political movement from the past, because as more Western thought and culture entered China, there was opposition to established political discourse and attitudes and new political problems arose. Once Deng Xiaoping stabilized his political power in the Party, he was concerned with advancing the cause of economic development announced at the Third Plenary Session of the Thirteenth Party Congress and at the same time sought to prevent attacks and subversion by bourgeois forces in ideology and the system. In the final analysis, he hoped to develop the economy under the control of the Communist Party, rather than pandering to the total questioning of the socialist system by activists. On October 12, 1983, he said at the second plenary meeting of the Twelfth Central Committee of the CPC: "In the ideological field there can be no spiritual pollution." He stressed: "The ideological battlefront is extensive and for now I only want to discuss theory and the literary and artistic fronts." He further hinted: "The essence of spiritual pollution is spreading the various kinds of decadent thinking of the bourgeois and other exploiting classes and distrust of the socialist and communist causes and the leadership of the Communist Party." He cited discussions on humanism, stressing the importance of the Marxist analysis of humanism and its "criticism of bourgeois humanism". He was very dissatisfied by some thinkers in the Party who "abstractly" discussed humanism, and expressed economic and political discontent with socialism using Marx's concept of "alienation" in their analysis; he held that the core of that theory was to "lead people to criticize, doubt, and reject socialism so that people lose confidence in the future of socialism and communism". Deng talked about art, and complained about literature and art that did not celebrate the Party and socialism and were "eager to describe darkness and grey areas". He also pointed out that "some people trumpet Western so-called 'modern' thought, openly proclaim that the highest purpose of literature and art is to 'express oneself', and disseminate an abstract theory of human nature and humanity". Deng noted the introduction of Western civilization into China after 1978 and emphasized the study of Western science, technology and management, but in the cultural field he stressed that "we must use Marxism to analyse, identify, and criticize their contents and methods". But "unanalysed, unidentified, and not criticized" phenomena are widespread, and he said that "the culture of the Western bourgeoisie in decline is corrupting our youth and can no longer be tolerated".

Most people in China were disgusted with politics and people's memories of the Cultural Revolution were still fresh; an emphasis on yet another political movement not only made people question the purposes of the new political group in power, but also severely shook people's confidence in participating in economic activities. At this time, opposition forces within the Party had been weakened and they could exert little pressure to induce the new collective leadership to abandon stepped up efforts to promote economic development. Therefore, the movement to oppose spiritual pollution lasted only a very short time, and in his government work report presented at the second meeting of the second session of the sixth National People's Congress on 15 May 1984, Zhao Ziyang announced:

> In the fight against spiritual pollution, because we begin by speaking unclearly in defining certain policies, some inappropriate things have occurred in some places and units, but once discovered, we will correct them in a timely manner.

In the end, this political campaign concluded after a little more than six months. A more open social life continued, and the policy of opening that had begun at the end of 1978 was only paused and not derailed by the campaign to "eliminate spiritual pollution"; according to the selection, translation, editing, and publication cycle, by 1984 many Western works continued to be translated and published, and one assumes these works had been analysed, identified, and criticized in accordance with Deng Xiaoping's wishes. Obviously, there were no legal provisions specifically limiting what publishers could select and review; "openness" and "ideological liberation" were legitimate bases for people's words and actions during this period and, therefore, more Western works were published over time and they occupied an increasingly large section of what was available in the market. This was the background that provided the soil for the so-called "85 Art Movement", and increasing numbers of young artists took the slogans and manifestos they used to defend their radical views from their reading of a large number of Western philosophers and thinkers including Nietzsche, Schopenhauer, Sartre, T. S. Eliot, and Freud. By the 1990s, and especially in the new century, Chinese translations of Western works could be seen everywhere, and the constant publication of new works did not attract any surprise.

Artists and critics who experienced the modernist movement of the 1980s all agree that the Rauschenberg exhibition at the National Art Museum of China (as well as in Lhasa) at the end of 1985 made a huge impact on them. Many years later, in June 2016, when the Ullens Center for Contemporary Art in Beijing's 798 Art District staged another Rauschenberg show, it was clear that artists and critics could not adequately pay tribute to the significance and influence that this American artist had exerted on Chinese modern art. Even though artists and critics might not have been clear about the background to Rauschenberg's use of "comprehensive" materials in the 1950s, the American artist's inclusion of paper, wood, glass, metal, and even stuffed animals in his work, which meant that painting lost its purity, was a liberating force for young Chinese. Li Xinjian, Rauschenberg's assistant at the time of his exhibition in Lhasa, commented:

> He was the first artist to bring so many of his works into the Chinese art scene, and this American contemporary pop art master engaged in face-to-face exchanges with Chinese artists. We can say that almost all contemporary artists in China at that time had him among their reference coordinates, and the American political term "cultural diplomacy" can be aptly used to describe Rauschenberg in China. The real outcome, in terms of background, means of expression, theory, and conceptual description, saw Chinese artists benefitting immensely from seeing an original artist from the West.[3]

In the mid-1980s, the various art phenomena that occurred in China under the influence of Western artistic ideas, styles, techniques, or concepts were summarized by critics as the "avant-garde" (*xianfeng yishu* or *qianwei yishu*) or "modern art" (*xiandai yishu*), and critics from the time defined the art of this period with such terms as the "85 Art Movement".[4] In any case, "rebellious" and "critical" positions constituted the subject of the new art from this period, and the ideological tools obviously came from the West. The basic techniques of culture and art were the metaphor, the allusion, and the symbol, and after socialist realism and its modes of expression were subjected to continuous criticism, almost no artist was willing to accept reflection theory and mimesis and use them to express their ideas. This endowed their works with a general obscurity and a lack of semantic clarity. Their artistic manifestos and statements were always filled with philosophical terms and even phrases, but to a great extent these did not let people know what the artist wanted to say. In this way, neither the language of art nor the ideas expressed in writing could be examined by censors imbued with official ideology.

On 10 June 1986, Deng Xiaoping said: "Now it looks as though we cannot adapt to the present situation if we do not engage in political reform. Reforms should include reform of the political system and political reform should serve as a symbol of reform." However, the demands for political reform in the intellectual world seem to have far exceeded those of the Party's leader. At the end of 1986 in Shanghai, Hefei, and other cities, student demonstrations and slogans had exceeded the limits imposed by the Chinese Communist Party, and in mid-December 1986, a number of university students from tertiary institutions in Shanghai, Nanjing, Hefei, Wuhan, Hangzhou, and Beijing took to the streets; in some schools posters of political dissent went up calling for the acceleration of the socialist democratic process and promoting the sensitive issue of political reform. On 16 January of the following year, at the enlarged meeting of the CPC, Party Secretary Hu Yaobang was subjected to political criticism and forced to resign from the post of General Secretary of the CPC Central Committee; on the 17th, the CPC's Anhui Provincial Committee decided to dismiss Fang Lizhi from the position of Vice-Chancellor of the University of Science and Technology of China, accusing him of inciting student demonstrations, denying socialism, and preaching bourgeois "democracy" and "freedom".[5] It was against this background that the Fourth New Figurative Exhibition organized by Zhang Xiaogang was prevented by the Sichuan Academy of Fine Arts from taking place.[6]

People's Daily representing the state ideology published an editorial entitled "Cherish and Develop the Political Situation of Stability and Unity" and commentary arguing that reform of the political system could only be conducted under the leadership of the Party. Shortly thereafter, on January 28, 1987, the CPC Central Committee issued a "Circular Addressing Current Issues Related to Combating Bourgeois

Liberalization".[7] In the sixth issue published in December that year, *Art Trends* gave notice to readers that it would cease publication with that issue.

In 1987 the political movement to oppose "bourgeois liberalization" did not last long because senior party leaders were determined to develop the economy and were worried by political movements (the historical experience of the period from 1949 to 1976 had made a deep impression on them) and the impact these could have on economic development. From party documents of 1987 and 1988, we can see that the pace of economic reform did not slacken because of radical political statements about the introduction of bourgeois capitalist thought, and this naturally opened up space for liberal ideas in culture and art. However, there was an obvious contradiction between using capitalist economic theory to develop the economy and not allowing bourgeois political thought and ethical spirit to affect Chinese thought. The solution was to speed up the development of the economy, and control as much as possible those university or intellectual circles whose words and deeds were not compatible with the Communist Party leadership. This is why intellectuals like Fang Lizhi were harshly criticized by official media and yet economic reform continued. In spite of official and academic circles from time to time issuing reminders that economic reform and political reform should be conducted in parallel, no sign of this happening could be seen. Anyway, theoretical statements could only address a minority, and even if the circular on opposing bourgeois liberalization issued by the CPC Central Committee on 28 January 1987 stressed that the core of bourgeois liberalization was "opposition to Party leadership" and that "the struggle against bourgeois liberal thought will be long-term", the document also issued a cautionary reminder that this political struggle was limited to the Party and "would not impact economic reform policy, rural policy, science and technology research, and technical exploration in literature and art, as well people's daily lives". The document specifically highlighted political strategy: "Combating bourgeois liberalization must be attentive to policy limits". Even if those Party members openly advocating bourgeois liberalization prove incorrigible or wish to develop their expertise, we respect their citizens' rights. At the same time, "we must prevent 'leftist' attacks on the 'right' in order to allow a hundred flowers bloom and a hundred schools of thought contend". Given the obvious lesson that people had been persecuted by political movements, the document stated: "The movement against bourgeois liberalization must adopt a correct approach, and not engage in a political campaign. We must adopt moderate, calm, and reasoned methods, be resolute in avoiding the past situation in which 'people were rigidly defined, pressure was exerted downwards, there were layers of investigation, and everyone had to pass muster', and call for the exposure of those who indulge in 'leftist' errors".

On 29 January, Zhao Ziyang at a Spring Festival gathering addressed people's concerns about the opposition to bourgeois liberalism:

> The "Announcement of the Enlarged Meeting of the Politburo of the CPC Central Committee" has been officially issued and urban and rural policies will remain unchanged. Comprehensive reforms will be unchanged, the policy of opening will be unchanged, stimulating the economy will be unchanged, and the policy of respecting knowledge and talented people will also remain unchanged; not only will these reforms remain intact, but we will also to try to do better.[8]

Because the reform of the commodity economy and changes in social life were so rapid, by 1987 one million farmers had already entered the capital from the countryside in search of work. The media also reported that there was a major trend of people going into business. In October that year, the CPC Central Committee, on their basis of their comparison and understanding of historical Chinese and foreign experience, simply determined that the system was the primary stage of socialism, which allowed for the further use of Western science and technology and economic methods. But this meant a strategic redefinition of the previously determined nature of the country's system and provided a stage for the later "socialist market economy"; at the same time, it also provided conditions for the further extension of their academic and intellectual logic. Ideological excitement was not stopped, but rather intensified by "opposition to bourgeois liberalization".

In *The History of Art in 20th-Century China*, there is a description of the context of the 1980s that serves to explain this:

> On January 1, 1988, Tiananmen Gate, a symbol of power and history, was open to the public for the first time. It was news that this historic site, still periodically used by politicians, was now open to the general public.

In contrast to this reassuring news, the New Year's Eve issue of *The World Economic Herald* carried an article entitled "The Most Important Issues for the Chinese Nation Are Global". Its author took this time of rest, the end of the year in the Chinese lunar calendar, to again focus attention on the country's crisis.[9] For more people, the serious events of the previous year showed the issues were more urgent than ever.

At the first meeting of the annual session of the Seventh National People's Congress in Beijing (25 March–13 April 1988), a constitutional amendment providing legal protection to the private economy was adopted.

On 26 April, the government designated Hainan as China's largest special economic zone, and outside all large companies and talent agencies, queues of hopeful employees rivalled in size those that had formed when more than 10 years prior it was announced that the Cultural Revolution work assignment situation had come to an end. Among young people at this time, starting a company or being employed by one was more than an economic act, but also a promise of liberation and an opportunity to participate in the trend of the times. Even though words like "business", "economy", and "the market" were words that alarmed and panicked intellectuals and scholars, by the second half of 1988, the "trend of commercialization" was passionately embraced by young people; this did not simply express their economic desires, but to a large extent expressed full-blown hope for the future.

In May, Deng Xiaoping discussed the risks of reform on two occasions, pointing out that reform and opening would have to negotiate some dangerous passages; even though people were concerned about prices, they would soon see that, as did even more intellectuals, that the risks were not only economic, but also political. In June, Deng Xiaoping, meeting with Czechoslovakian guests, said: "Science and technology are the primary productive force." People's objectives were guided by national leaders as much as possible towards technical areas, so that political problems were replaced by technical problems in the name of productivity. In July, the CPC Central Committee issued a circular announcing that the discipline inspection groups of the Party in the various government departments would be phased out. The circular announcing the revocation of the Party's role in the government sector was an important measure of political reform, and these measures prompted sensitive intellectuals to point out that the possibility of upheaval was likely to increase in the political arena; the political reality was full of more challenges than the "opposition to bourgeois liberalization" one year prior.

Around 1988, a large quantity of political reporting addressing such issues as liberty, "sacrosanct Party doctrine", changes in gender relations, the Tangshan earthquake, links formed by globalization, problems related to abortion, and the issue of national strengthening passionately and romantically articulated popular political issues, and their authors and avid readers were engaged with reality and a new understanding of traditional culture. Moreover, in June and August 1988 this liberating and aggressive new mentality found its highest expression in a six-episode CCTV-2 television series providing political commentary entitled *River Elegy*.

On 11 June 1988 the public reaction to the premiere screening of the six-part documentary was unprecedented. People long familiar with eulogies of the cultural images provided by the "Yellow River" and "the dragon" now encountered the identification of these images as forces or incarnations of evil by the young scholars who wrote the material for the series: Su Xiaokang, Xie Xuanjun, Yuan Zhiming, and Zhang Gang. The "dragon" was described in the commentary as "a monster that was an image of violence", and this "monster" had become the symbol of China's rulers, while the Yellow River was not only associated with authoritarian rule but with what was old and worn out.

In fact, in the 1980s, Chinese intellectuals were well aware of the nature of the Chinese state and its political reality through their reading of translated and imported Western philosophy and ideas; since the aging yellow dragon with its monstrous influence continued to dominate the nation, it was easy to deduce that the nature of the country was authoritarian. Authors were already familiar with the key words in these arguments and they had simply not previously been so publicly articulated.[10]

Apart from presenting the Great Wall not as a symbol of ancient Chinese civilization and its brilliant history but as a direct indictment of cringing before foreigners (in the second episode entitled "Destiny"), *River Elegy* also accused China's traditional political culture of contempt for science (in the third episode entitled "Light"), pointing out that the outbreak of the Russian Revolution of 1917 signalled by the firing of the cannon on the cruiser Aurora would in fact provide no fundamental solution for the development problems of socialist national economies (in the fourth episode entitled "The New Era"):

> The "Stalinist model" which once applied to all countries of Eastern Europe led, sooner or later, to "dissidence" and the implementation

> of reforms. The rise of an independent Yugoslavia in the Balkans first broke with the Soviet model and explored its own path. Later Hungary, Poland, and Czechoslovakia all underwent transformation and took to the road of reform. History seemed to raise Plekhanov's doubts once again.[11]

At this time, scholars still rejoiced when even small reforms were announced, as when Communist Party Chief Zhao Ziyang, speaking on behalf of the CPC, acknowledged in a speech that the "commodity economy" was a rational aspect of the socialist economy. Intellectuals borrowed the explanations of the economist Li Yining, a professor at Peking University, in discussing questions of change in the system of ownership:

> As I said, the failure of economic reform may be due to failure of price reform, and the success of China's economic reforms will depend on the success of reforming the system of ownership. Addressing the key issue of reform of the system of ownership must challenge our concept of traditional public ownership; we must transform traditional public ownership into a new public ownership system.[12]

Obviously, up until this time, economists as intellectuals tactfully avoided terminology fraught with political risks. But in any case, what the intellectuals were saying could be understood by anyone: the social system of the country needed to be changed.

In the sixth episode of *River Elegy* entitled "The Colour Blue", Bao Zunxin, a researcher at the Chinese Academy of Social Sciences, editor of the *Culture and Philosophy* book series and editor-in-chief of *Research on the History of Chinese Philosophy*, again highlighted the importance of the "democratic spirit" and the "spirit of science" of the May Fourth period. On 7 December 1988, Jin Guantao, an adviser at Peking University's Institute of the Future, held a seminar on "China and the World" at which he noted in his address to the plenary session: "The experiment of socialism and its failure are the two major legacies of the 20th century".[13] At this time, there was also a flurry of books, journals, and articles that treated acute social problems. There was a prevailing sense of general crisis: the contradictions between rapid economic growth and slow political reform were becoming more prominent, and several years of development of market economy mechanisms were further disrupting the established order of society. Disturbing phenomena began to emerge in the wake of reforms: millions of the rural population had abandoned agricultural production in their desire to enter the big cities; some factories were bankrupt, others had insufficient work, and the prospect of an army of tens of millions of unemployed led people to panic; poor railway traffic management was resulting in frequent accidents; university campuses were characterized by an atmosphere of absurdity, indifference, superficiality, decadence, and alarm; and coupled with inflation, official corruption was prevalent. All this constituted an unbearable psychological burden on people.

In a book entitled *China's Crisis and Thinking* published in February 1989, its editor Li Ming's anxiety was exhaustively revealed in the four sub-headings he included in his preface ("tragedy", "crisis", "the tragic consciousness of crisis" and "China's crisis"). In his preface, the editor expressed the general view of radical intellectuals:

> China's contemporary crises, deposited by history and stemming from reality, have spread to all psychological, physical, and social areas, penetrating all levels covered by phenomenology, structuralism, and deconstruction. Inflation, rising prices, food shortages, and so on, can be said to constitute the most immediate and most urgent crisis. However, the deep crisis in Chinese psychology, morality, beliefs, and values is often injurious and destructive, and there is a serious lack of social power; the most profound crisis is in education, study seems useless, there is tiredness in teaching, and illiteracy is spreading, all of which is really worrying for the future of China. The crisis in the political system

> of China stems from following the tradition of the old system, which still plays an important role. In Chinese culture elements that are old, antiquated, anti-intellectual, anti-liberal, anti-modern, anti-democratic, and anti-scientific await further reform, and because Chinese society tends towards disorder, these often result in obstructive polarizing turbulence that is at the root of extremely slow social development.

In art circles, some critics in 1985 and 1986 tired of the modernist movement, and questioning the influence to date of Western "avant-garde" art on some questions of art, they hoped at least for a decisive change in artistic language, not a shoddy imitation of Western modern art. No one directly opposed such judgments, but most people wanted to discard the intellectual dichotomy between language and form: there was no problem with the spirit and stance of content, but there was a problem with how language could respond and creatively echo the problem. However, critics who advocated "language purification" could cite no good examples of what they were calling for; an academic classical style of painting was used instead as an example of linguistic purification and, as a result, the discussion lost direction. Being a political activist, the critic Li Xianting (writing under the pseudonym "Hu Cun") published an article, "Our Times Await the Fervor of the Grand Soul", that sparked debate among artists and critics (*Fine Arts in China*, 1988:37). In this article, he presented his concept of the "grand soul":

> The soul of our times has taken shape as a result of the dramatic cultural collision between East and West and the enormous contrasts between those who are advanced and those who are retrograde. In the deep recesses of this grand soul, endless uncertainty rolls about violently: hope and despair interweave, ideals and reality are in contradiction, the tradition and the future are in conflict, while pain, anxiety, hesitation, and all manner of suffering accompany reflections on culture as ideas are tossed back and forth.

In the later part of the essay, Li Xianting explained that an artist "must at a timely juncture appreciate that this soul is more important than his own personal soul". He attributed his idea to T. S. Eliot. Li Xianting's explanation might have been suitable for the earlier modernist movement, as well as for the post-1978 Scar Art; what mattered was not the question of language, but the rush and impact of the "grand soul". In the view of Li Xianting, the "grand soul" of avant-garde art would disappear if language were "purified": "the current 'purification of language' potential ran the greatest risk of a return to the days of psychological evasion and whitewashing". When Li Xianting discussed the value of the works of the great early masters, they were not all defined by the language paradigms and techniques of the exhibited works, but the soul later ascribed to them, and thus he concluded: what is "behind" these masters' works is more important than the works themselves. He stated:

> There is nothing more tragic for the artist than to have too much placed on him, which makes the artist measure himself against all the masters in the entire history of art, rather than experiencing the pain felt in the living world. Once language, skill, and style become the artist's goals, artists become just like workers who have to go to work, and under the guise of "autonomy" art loses its self-contained life and impulse.

Li Xianting's logic was that when artistic practice was separate from language, language "purification" or refinement was probably impossible. Li Xianting in this passage is clear: art must continue to perform its critical mission.

As early as the first half of 1986, Li Xianting published an article in Fine Arts in China (1986: 28) entitled "It's Not the Art That's Important". This article sought to make people aware that the new wave artists and their work had true value and should engage our empathy:

> We can see in many of their works that their anxiety and their confusion derive from their re-examination of all concepts

in which human values are central, and so they preferred modern Western philosophy, like writing polemical articles, and took pleasure in abstruse and abstract expression. This indicated that the movement of emancipation in thought had begun to enter the stage of philosophy. But this was not the modern art movement itself and at best only a preparatory stage in ideas, because their poverty in science and philosophy forced them to pretend to be philosophers. The weakness of their ideas meant that their works of art could not sustain the heavy responsibility demanded of them, yet they had to shoulder this heavy thought, and this was the pride, as well as the tragedy, of Chinese contemporary art.

The *China/Avant-garde: China Modern Art Exhibition* that opened on 5 February 1989 at the National Art Museum of China was a symbol of its time, and all the radical performances at the exhibition and their consequences were a symbol of the period and marked the end of radical modernism. Of course, the exhibition organizers or curators had envisaged something quite different, most of the audience and those involved in art were thrilled and stimulated by such dramatic performance works as Li Shan's *Washing Feet*, Zhang Nian's *Incubating Eggs*, and Xiao Lu's *Dialogue*.[14]

Ideological conflict and increasing excitement also exacerbated the imminent explosion of the social and political crises. On 16 February during the *China Modern Art Exhibition*, the political radical Chen Jun gave a press conference for foreign journalists at JJ's Art Bar, and distributed Fang Lizhi's letter to Deng Xiaoping and the open letter of 33 people to the National Standing Committee and CPC Central Committee calling for the implementation of an amnesty and the release of Wei Jingsheng and other political prisoners; on 22 March the 12th Democracy Salon was held at Peking University by Fang Lizhi, Li Shuxian, and Wang Dan. Professors at Peking University gave lectures on the topic of "New Authoritarianism and Democracy"; "democracy" and "human rights" were concepts frequently invoked in salons. On 5 April, at the 14th Democracy Salon, 56 students from different colleges signed a poster calling for political democracy, and the student Wang Dan suggested: "All intellectuals feel something will happen this year, and I hope that soon everyone will come together." On 15 April, China Central Television broadcast the notice from the Chinese Communist Party Central Committee that Hu Yaobang had died. That night, a large poster appeared at Peking University: "We request that the incompetent government be removed, the autocratic monarchy be overthrown, and democracy be established". On 16 April, wreaths opened on the Heroes Monument in Tiananmen Square; on 18 April, more than 1,000 students from Peking University began walking from the campus to Tiananmen Square. Thereafter, in the name of honouring Hu Yaobang, the numbers of students marching to the Square increased daily until there were tens of thousands and then hundreds of thousands demonstrating in the Square. They shouted various different slogans. On 22 April, three students at the East Gate of the Great Hall of the People requested that they be allowed to present a petition to Prime Minister Li Peng. The events in Tiananmen Square had become the focus of global media attention. On 25 April, CCTV News aired the following day's People's Daily editorial, entitled "We Must Unequivocally Oppose the Turmoil", which unequivocally opposed the student voices and demonstrations. On the 28th, the "Beijing University Student Government Association" comprising representatives of more than 20 higher educational institutions was established. More frequent militant activities and political risks were taken by the demonstrators. By 19 May, when the Square still contained nearly 100,000 people, the Politburo decided that night to impose martial law the next day. From 20 May martial law was implemented, and at 1:30 a.m. on 4 June, troops cleared Tiananmen Square. What unfolded in Tiananmen Square spread to other cities in China, until the country was engulfed in a full-scale political crisis.

Most modern artists felt despondent and depressed by events in the second half of 1989. The artist Zhang Xiaogang wrote in a letter to his friend in the United

States Yang Qian: "I am often woken up by nightmares and reawaken to the great tragedy that surrounds us. On the one hand we now have a clear understanding of reality, on the other we feel deeply confused about the future." He complained about the domestic situation and the school at the end of the letter: "At times I feel that there can really be no purpose in life for this generation, but nature hasn't caved in so maybe this is my life."[15] At the end of the year, Zhang Xiaogang again described his feelings to Yang Qian:

> The 1990s is coming soon and for the last decade of the century, people will never escape the fear. I more often have nightmares, and combined with the constant winter rain in Chongqing and power outages, sometimes people feel desperate. I am looking forward to the end of this cold, wet winter.[16]

In 1990, Zhang Xiaogang, in a letter to his friend Yi Dan, reported on the situation among the teachers at the Sichuan Academy of Fine Arts in the Huangjueping district of Chongqing:

> It is the 1990s. On the last night of 1989, we gathered listlessly at Ye Yongqing's house, talked in a desultory way about the weather and the Tuopai spirits challenge. After listening to the New Year ring in, I went home to sleep. For the past few months, sleep and nightmares have become synonymous

> for me. I believe that everyone is waiting for something to happen – it might be an earthquake or perhaps a visitation of fairies.[17]

Nothing better describes the psychological situation at that time: everything had ended and everyone was waiting for someone to kick off the next day. Throughout 1990, with the exception of those artists and critics who had left the country, those who continued to live in different cities in China felt they were subject to an unprecedented listless and helpless mental state: the age of ideological excitement had ended.

Notes

1. Gao Minglu et al., "Avant Garde Art and Cultural Reality", *Reading*, Beijing, 1989, 5th issue.

2. Liu Xun (1923-2007), born in Nanjing, Jiangsu, painter, Vice President and Secretary of the Beijing Painting Academy, Vice President of the Beijing Artists' Association. He joined the Communist Party at an early date, entered Northern Shaanxi Public School, and did further studies at the Lu Xun Academy in Yan'an. In 1945 he went to work in the liberated areas of Northeast China as a war reporter and editor of *Northeast Pictorial*. After 1949, he became editor-in-chief of *People's Pictorial*, editor-in-chief of People's Fine Arts Publishing House's *Lianhuanhua Bao*, and chief art editor at People's Fine Arts Publishing House. In the Anti-Rightist Movement he was classified as a "rightist", and during the Cultural Revolution he endured nine years' imprisonment.

3. Xu Liang, interview with Li Xinjian, *World Art*, May 2008.

4. Gao Minglu described the art of this period as the "85 Art Movement" in a talk at the National Oil Painting Art Seminar in April, 1986.

5. In January, the writer Wang Ruowang and the Vice Chairman of China Writers' Association, Liu

Binyan, were also expelled from the Party. Previously, on December 30, Deng Xiaoping told Hu Yaobang and others: "I read Fang Lizhi's speech and it was not like a speech by a Communist Party member. Such people should not remain in the Party, but should be expelled." Deng said that the student protests of the last few years made it clear that the tide of bourgeois liberalism must be opposed resolutely. "I haven't given up the fight against spiritual pollution and I agree that the full text of my speech at the second plenary session should be included in my collected works. We must fight bourgeois liberalization for at least another 20 years." See: Central Documentation Publishing House ed., *Chronicle of Deng Xiaoping*, 2004, pp. 1160-1162.

6. At the end of 1986, Zhang Xiaogang began preparations at the Sichuan Academy of Fine Arts for the fourth New Figurative exhibition. This was the later phase of the so-called "85 Art Movement". Previously, in April, the Oil Painting Art Committee had sponsored the National Oil Painting Art Seminar (14-17 April) and had invited avant-garde artists and critics including Zhang Peili, Shu Qun, Li Shan, Zhu Qingsheng, and Gao Minglu to participate. Although such older artists as Zhan Jianjun, Wen Lipeng, Wu Zuoren, Luo Gongliu, and Wu Guanzhong participated in the Seminar, they allowed Gao Minglu to give an academic report on the 85 Art Movement, and slides of several hundred new works, including New

Perceptual works, were shown. This event obviously fired the enthusiasm of the young people who wanted society and the art world to understand the new art, and it also later encouraged the New Figurative artists to organize exhibitions and other activities. Earlier in June, when they heard that a modernist group in Chengdu called "Red, Yellow and Blue" was organizing an exhibition, Zhang Xiaogang made enquiries and suggested to Zhou Chunya that they hold a three-man (Zhou Chunya, Zhang Xiaogang, Ye Yongqing) exhibition in Chengdu. At that time, new wave art was spreading through the cities of China, enthusing Zhang Xiaogang about organizing the fourth *New Figurative* exhibition at the Sichuan Academy of Fine Arts. In a letter to Ye Yongqing dated 1 December 1986, Zhang cheerfully described his exhibition program: "The program I am planning will be a three-day art event at the end of this month, similar to an art festival. The main activities will be: (1) A display of photographs of our works and texts, which Yin Qiong already supports. This will be a daytime event. (2) We will ask activists (in philosophy, literature, and photography) from other schools to come and organize seminars. This is more or less organized. (3) We will let the students put on a modernist drama written, directed, and played by the students. This might be more difficult. (4) A slide night. If you agree with the idea, we could show the photographs we took in Xishuangbanna, and give a leisurely explanation of the customs, religion, and so on."

Unfortunately, an imminent nationwide political campaign against "bourgeois liberalization" had been announced by the Communist Party and all independent activities and debate at schools and academic institutions were proscribed. The Sichuan Academy of Fine Arts was quick to implement the orders issued by the Communist Party and Zhang Xiaogang was told that he would be unable to include any of planned recitation events in the event he was organizing. On 28 December, Zhang sent a report on the progress he was making with his exhibition to Mao Xuhui and Ye Yongqing in Kunming. At the start of the letter he gave a resolute and spirited account of his planning and design of the art events, and wrote that "the moribund posturing of the Academy of Fine Arts failed to dent" the exhibition and art activities that had been enthusiastically arranged. Zhang Xiaogang described the event: "The upshot was that many people attended the event, both Chinese and foreigners, and some people waited for the exhibition to open from the early hours of the morning. The leaders of the Academy and a number of shady people also filed through the exhibition, which was unprecedented." In the end, however, the fourth *New Figurative* exhibition did not go according to plan, as Zhang Xiaogang described in a subsequent letter of 28 December:

> Starting from the first day, the leaders summoned me for a talk and on the morning of the next day, the people from the Party office again summoned me for a talk! The

reason was simple; the campus unrest in Shanghai had been spread by students from Shanghai who had come to Chongqing, where students now wanted to hold a street demonstration. This was bad timing and I had never expected that the school would now be watching me almost as though I was public enemy number one. In addition our partners, the members of the Chongqing Teachers College Literary Society, suddenly left without warning yesterday morning, pulling the rug out from under us, and the people who were going to present lectures (also from Chongqing Teachers College) scheduled for eight o'clock in the evening did not turn up. I had prepared everything and there were already a lot of people sitting in the auditorium; at the same time, behind the stage curtain, the Communist Party Secretary of the Academy was presiding over a meeting he had convened of the Communist Youth League's Student Union to discuss the question of the student movement. At the same time, other people were all suddenly disappearing! I felt so isolated!" (Provided by Ye Yongqing)

7. Previously, on 13 January 1987, Deng Xiaoping met with Japan LDP Secretary-General Takeshita and

said the recent "student unrest" "had little attraction for students." He said:

> This was a big mistake. We must take a clear-cut stand, change those being misled, educate young people with our own history, and expose those people with ulterior motives, because their slogans are against the leadership of the Communist Party, opposed to the socialist road. [...] These people advocate total Westernization and want to bring Western capitalism to China. These agitators are well-known people, and we have to deal with these people.
> *Uphold the Four Cardinal Principles and Combat Bourgeois Liberalization*, People's Publishing House, February 1987.

8. *Uphold the Four Cardinal Principles and Combat Bourgeois Liberalization*, People's Publishing House, February 1987, p. 394.

9. The text of the article was strident:

> From overall economic strength, especially per capita indicators, it can be said, the Chinese people once again "face great danger", the danger being no less than that of the life and death time when our anthem *March of the Volunteers* was written. If current rates continue, in about 50 or 60 years, China will reproduce the

> conditions when foreigners used cannons against us in the Opium War, and we Chinese had only swords and spears. If we lack awareness about this situation […] our country and people may fall behind, and there will be no ranking for us in the world.

This radical statement in the context of the discussion of globalization turned what were considered to be economic problems into political problems, and the crisis of national survival was reduced to political systems and ideologies. By the end of April, its radical positions led to the newspaper ceasing publication.

10. The authors' views and stance called for changing the existing political system. In 1988, Hong Kong's *Liberation Monthly* (November issue) ran an article entitled "The Devil Incarnate Mao Zedong" by Liu Xiaobo that expressed very clearly these political attitudes and goals:

> China's reality hinges on this: No force can be found within authoritarianism to oppose authoritarianism. Specifically, in politics the strength cannot be found within a one-party dictatorship to oppose one-party dictatorship; economically, within the economy of public ownership and the planned economy the momentum to reform cannot be found; in terms of ideology, new ideas cannot be found

in Marxist doctrine; in the broader culture, nothing excellent can be found within traditional Chinese culture. Only multiparty democracy can replace one-party dictatorship, only private ownership can replace public ownership and only the market economy can replace the planned economy; only a diversity of ideas and freedom of expression and thought can replace monistic thought; only modern world (Western) culture can replace traditional Chinese culture.

11. Cui Wenhua ed., *Discussion of River Elegy*, Culture and Arts Publishing House, 1988, p. 42.

12. Cui Wenhua ed., *Discussion of River Elegy*, Culture and Arts Publishing House, 1988, p. 51.

13. See: General Office of the Beijing Municipal Committee of the CPC ed., *Record of the 1989 Suppression of the Counter-revolutionary Turmoil in Beijing* (1989 Beijing zhizhi dongluan pingxi fangeming baoluan jishi), Beijing Daily Press, August 1989. A few months later, the political actions of the scholars and other intellectuals who participated in the 4 June political events inevitably prejudiced their political and intellectual positions.

14. At around 10:00 a.m. on the 11th, Xiao Lu fired a shot at her installation work. The "shot" led to the

exhibition being closed for the first time. On 10 February, the exhibition reopened. On 14 February, the *Beijing Daily*, Beijing Public Security Bureau, and National Art Museum of China simultaneously received an anonymous letter threatening that explosive devices had been placed at premises of these three organisations and the China Modern Art Exhibition was immediately shut down. For safety, the China Art Gallery was closed for two days. On 17 February, the exhibition opened again and ended on 19 February.

15. "Letter to Yang Qian from Zhang Xiaogang (6 October)", in Zhang Xiaogang, Lü Peng ed., *Amnesia and Memory: Zhang Xiaogang's Correspondence, 1981-1996*, Peking University Press, 2010, pp. 139-140.

16. "End of year letter to Yang Qian from Zhang Xiaogang", in Zhang Xiaogang, Lü Peng ed., *Amnesia and Memory: Zhang Xiaogang's Correspondence, 1981-1996*, Peking University Press, 2010, p. 142.

17. "Letter to Yi Dan from Zhang Xiaogang (9 January)", in Zhang Xiaogang, Lü Peng ed., *Amnesia and Memory: Zhang Xiaogang's Correspondence, 1981-1996*, Peking University Press, 2010, p. 150.

History as Tactics

In a country under the control of an individual's will and authority, this control will determine the scope of the basic words and actions of everyone living in this country. An individual, in the face of pressure from society and the state, will usually protect themselves in a tortuous manner or simply change his perception of reality; this is the result of the necessity of survival and there will be a struggle to find blind spots within a space. In the final analysis, the maximum self-expression will be limited by conditions: this is the instinct of life.

Between 1978 and 1989, despite the emergence of short-lived political movements to "eliminate spiritual pollution" and "oppose bourgeois liberalization", most of the time translations of Western thought (politics, economics, philosophy, religion, literature, art, and other humanities) filled the schools (tertiary institutions by and large) and institutions in which intellectuals were concentrated. As can be imagined, the result was that Western thought exerted growing influence, especially on the political system, philosophical concepts, and the fields of literature and art. This led to doubts concerning existing politics, and this was attributed in the main to "spiritual pollution" and "bourgeois liberalization". In parallel with the development of the commodity economy, the question of how to stop people from adopting the entire bourgeois ideology that favoured the market economy was not an easy thing, unless the door was again closed to contact with the outside world.

However, from the outset Deng Xiaoping was not able to draw the line at the overall situation of studying the West or found it difficult to filter Western influences while still preserving what was required from the West. For example, limited technical knowledge was required to develop the commodity economy, while filtering out political thought that could destabilize the leadership of the party and change the nature of society. On 12 September 1988, in listening to a report on prices and their initial program of reform, Deng continued to express optimism about economic development, telling his Party colleagues: "Controlling inflation and price rises cannot damage our reform and opening-up policy and cannot make the economy shrink, so we must maintain a proper pace of development". However, after 15 April 1989 the social atmosphere made the Party uneasy, and people commemorating Hu Yaobang's death were expressing dissatisfaction with the Party. Discussing the students and people gathering in Tiananmen Square in Beijing on 25 April, Deng told Li Peng and Yang Shangkun at his residence: "This is not a student movement, this is chaos. It is crystal clear that we must take effective measures to oppose and suppress this unrest." Deng said: "The aim of these people is to overthrow Communist Party leadership." He complained that "the earlier opposition to bourgeois liberalization had not been followed through on, and that the campaign against spiritual pollution was abandoned after a little more than 20 days. If it had been carried out effectively, thinkers and educators wouldn't have found themselves in this mess."[1]

However, after June, Deng Xiaoping repeatedly stressed the importance of economic development in different places, and in early 1992, after examining economic development in Shanghai and Guangdong's coastal cities, he could see the results of the development of the commodity economy over the previous decade as well as the real confidence in these places in the market economy. On 12 June, Deng Xiaoping at his place of residence told Party Secretary Jiang Zemin that he was all in favour of the "socialist market economy": "With what we are actually doing, Shenzhen is a socialist market economy." Earlier during his trip to the South he warned those who were suspicious of the market economy to not use the terms "socialist" or "capitalist" in their writings, adding that "while there might be more planning, this was not the essential difference between socialism and capitalism; the planned economy was not equivalent to socialism, and capitalism also has planning; the market economy is not capitalism, because socialism also has markets".[2]

Deng repeatedly stressed the importance of the Party's leadership, but the aim was to develop what he called a "socialist economy". Until then, people had a basic belief: if politics did not matter and the focus was on the market, it might be possible to gain material wealth as well as access to security, and creating material wealth was the most basic and important part of people's work and daily lives. Isn't our fight for democracy to get more material goods? Isn't ideological liberation intended to better develop the economy? Most people also followed this logic of the Party in understanding reality. In theory, no one has conditions to discuss the relationship between political reform and economic reform, since the core leadership of the Party had set the basic tone: one centre and two basic points. The central task was economic construction, and the two points were adhering to the four cardinal principles and the reform and opening.[3]

From June 1989 to October 1992, the number of exhibitions of modern or contemporary art could be counted on the fingers of one hand, and some small modern art exhibitions were held in underground spaces. Most of the critics and artists who had not left the country were living in a miasma of hopelessness. The ideological thrust was over, and for activists, there was no path to success and so a rethink was required for those who wanted to go on. It was now clear that new possibilities were presented by the market, and even though the art market had been subject to criticism and suppression by Mao Zedong since 1949, the market which had long been considered to be the basic characteristic of capitalist society had now achieved legal status in China. In that case, people began to acquire a vague understanding of the rules of the game determining the market economy; nothing had changed, except that "economic development" was now clearly expressed as the development of the "market economy". It was in this context that in January 1991 the first issue of a journal devoted to the art market, called simply *Art·Market*, was published in China. In the foreword of that journal, the editor intentionally steered clear of ideological disputes and announced that the journal's focus was on the market and the goal was developing an art market that acquired a new legitimacy:

> After ten years of economic reform and development, China's unique model of development and the rapidity of change have won the attention of the international community. In this, people pay attention to how this reflects aspects of the Chinese nation's spirit, philosophy, morality, and the aesthetic sense of art and culture. In the last ten years China's art has, through exhibitions, publications, and other forms, increasingly influenced the world, in the same way that corresponding forms of Western art and other foreign cultures have been widely introduced and spread in China. Eastern and Western societies have never at any time had such frequently and mutually beneficial contacts as at present, and mutual, interactive and penetrating criticism in politics, economics, and especially culture will constitute the existence of a new humanity. In such a context, only something like "commercialized culture"

> (*jingjihua wenhua*) can more accurately describe the contemporary culture of our times; Chinese contemporary art is adopting unsophisticated forms and channels to enter the international cycle of "the art industry", despite the fact that few people are acutely aware of this. However, because of this, it is crucial for a correct understanding and participation that leading museums, galleries, collectors, art dealers, art dealers, art publishers, and intermediaries have the information that will benefit the development of art. We know that art in contemporary society faces a different situation from art in other times, in that its value has to be fully reflected through price, even though the value of art is not economic in the sense of price. In this regard, the sale of artworks is the basic premise or guarantee for the efficacy and significance of the work of artists and art dealers, galleries and museums, not to mention art intermediaries. In today's society, it is inconceivable that a culture lacking in "economic clout" can be effective.

In 1991 official statements relating to the market remained vague, and only a few people in the art world could mentally link art and the market, but many critics were involved in the art market and in art and discussed market issues.

In genial discussions of the relationship between art and the market, the critic Huang Zhuan in his essay titled "Who Will Sponsor History?" pursued the question of the art history that created the art market. He reminded people to pay attention to the writing of art history, and wrote about a common cognitive bias:

> For a long time, our art history has fabricated many myths about how artists become great because of a unique and innate obsession, but it rarely relates how each artist has acquired fame because of extremely complex modes of reality, how behind and around them various political and religious forces, various aesthetic groups, art brokers, painting businessmen, people taking orders, collectors, and critics have played a subtle and immeasurable role in the process of history. It should be said that all of these forces are supporters of art history, and are also a part of the history of art.[4]

In this way, ideology and style have long been popular in China, and in the history of art, especially in the writing of the history of contemporary art, this has been seriously questioned. Huang Zhuan cited the example of the formation in China of the myth of Van Gogh in the 1980s as an example, and he tried to throw a basin of cold water over those with no knowledge of history who blindly accepted the myth of Van Gogh: "Such cynical philistines will remain failures all their lives. An artist who only sold his works for low prices during his lifetime is now the best selling artist in the Western art market, yet history recognizes him only in terms of eight figure prices. Of course, you can say that Eight-Figure van Gogh is so great, but I want to get away from the art scene that discusses the greatness of an art work or artist in such unforeseeable terms." Throughout the 1980s, Irving Stone's biography of Van Gogh *Lust for Life* was very popular among young artists, and most young Chinese poeticized and romanticized Van Gogh's pain and anxiety, and how his art derived from his destitution and utter poverty and from his suffering in life; that's the life that produced such great art. However, Huang Zhuan also pointed out that the myth of capitalism comes from capital. When an editor asked him about "the modes of historicizing art and artists in our time", Huang replied:

> Someone interested in this question might be better going through art magazines produced in the United States and Taiwan and reading about gallery owners like Leo Castelli and corporate collectors like Morishita Yasumichi. As an art businessman, Castelli is described in the Western art scene as the "pope of contemporary art" and as someone who "wrote history"; this is not simply because from the late 1950s on, he launched through his gallery the likes of such masters that represent an era as

Rauschenberg, Jasper Johns, Frank Stella, Lichtenstein, and Warhol, but also because he applied commercial power successfully to create a mode of historicizing art works and artists. Obviously, any history of post-war art must mention Castelli, just as it would be impossible to write about the art of the Middle Ages without mentioning the Christian Church, the art of Michelangelo without mentioning the Medici family or the Pope, or the history of Chinese literati paintings without mentioning such leaders of interest groups as Su Shi and Dong Qichang. I believe that if Castelli the patron of art history emerged today, he would be fundamentally associated with the economy of human life and, as Marx said, we should consider this reality from an economic basis. In these times of high-level industrialization, human economic and commercial activities have more significance for human civilization and human behaviour; the biggest difference between modern economics and classical economics is that the former begins with the behaviour of human culture as a whole rather than and not simply from the people and things of benefit to economic activity in the human pursuit of profit-maximizing behaviour.[5]

That statement emphasizes that economic forces may be a human instinct at the present time. This is an age in which the Centre clearly promotes the market economy; in cities like Shenzhen and Guangzhou that were China's earliest reform and opening cities, there is no shame associated with words like "sale", "trade", or "making money". Art, if required, can also be an exchange of goods. However, Shenzhen and Guangzhou are viewed in China as a "cultural desert", this means that people in the two cities lack an understanding and awareness of art, not to mention the ideological positions concealed within a work of art. The background also means that those modernist works can escape from the political oversight of official ideology in a city that does not understand culture or art. In fact, in official vetting of exhibitions by the local Department of Culture, eight works by Wang Guangyi from his *Great Criticism* series that included his *Marlboro* works were, as in the rest of China, not allowed to be shown, but because the ideology of the market prevails and is supported in Guangzhou, the artist was able to apply, pay a fee, and have the decision overturned.[6]

In short, Huang Zhuan at this time felt keenly that "the commercialization of serious works of art, or the establishment of an art market with true meaning, allows us essentially to appreciate the world significance in the history of modern art".[7]

An artist, unlike a critic, is not concerned with rational discourse, and artists instinctively perceive, and respond to, new things. When Wang Guangyi responded to questions about money, he had this to say:

> I am an artist, and I believe money and art are good things. Only after thousands of years did humans discover that only art and money could bring joy and contemplation. As an artist I love money like ordinary people, but unlike ordinary people who use money to live a luxurious life, an artist uses money to maintain a mythic image. The more awesome the myth of an artist, the more valuable his works are. Within this, the metaphysics of a myth has the function of converting a mundane myth into a rule. The relationship between these two aspects mutually advances the art process, and it should be said that the negative and positive aspects of these "Matthew effects" phenomena in contemporary art enclose the birth and death of the myth of artists, critics and the art market.[8]

Even when discussing mundane problems, Wang Guangyi also tends to use wise words that draw towards the metaphysical nature of the problem.

Older artists had a somewhat different reaction to the market; from the outset they kept a wary eye on the market, as is evident from He Duoling's answer to an interviewer's question:

> I do want to be around markets and I am not able to do a boss's bidding. So far I have not had a boss who wants me to paint this or that. They've all said to me: paint what you want. Of course some bosses will say they like something or that this has a certain effect when they are offering advice, but I usually ignore this. Even if the work can't sell, I will try a different way of making money.[9]

He Duoling was dealing with something quite different from the Castelli-style commercial galleries, but he still used the word "exploitation", as when he said: "My painting *Little Di* sold in Japan for USD 16,000, but most of that went to the exhibition organizers so that after I only received CNY 13,000, which for me is an example of exploitation." The uncertainty of the art market made him feel uncomfortable, so that he even thought of buying back paintings he had sold, although he was never faced with having to put this idea into practice.

Zhang Peili, a major conceptual artist, when asked about the relationship between art and money, answers in a way that is as obscure as his art works. He said that "commercialization" made him think of "alienation". Obviously, he had not thought deeply about the question of what society was without "alienation". The concept had emerged in the 1980s in the course of intellectual debates about early Marxism and here the artist must have viewed "alienation" as something negative and disagreeable. In discussing the commercialization of art, he said:

> There is no denying that business enables the realization of today's art projects, such as Walter De Maria's *Vertical Earth Kilometre*, and this cannot be regarded as something that many people would have found reassuring. But the business community benefited contemporary art in its attack on other current art, although the influence remained rather subdued.[10]

Zhang Peili had no confidence in the art market per se and was very wary about art market trends, and in this he was more anxious about the dissipation of the significance of art than his classmate Wang Guangyi. He said: "The great temptation with commercialization is that few people care about the loss of meaning, and more people unreservedly accept an alienated reality. A result of this change is that at the same time that contemporary art has developed, it has lost its positive spirit and vitality."[11]

In the early 1990s as the market atmosphere intensified, Shao Dazhen, professor of art history at the Central Academy of Art, also discussed the art market in the pages of *Art·Market*. Citing the experiences of Rembrandt, Vermeer, and Van Gogh as examples, he explained how art prices and value are likely to be asymmetrical. He expressed a hope that "the demarcation lines between exploratory and academic art and the so-called 'commercial' would become increasingly faint, until they disappear, and at that time people could determine the selling price of artworks in line with true value".[12]

Prior to the 1990s, the Chinese art world had almost no contact with the market, and so naturally could not anticipate the difficult problems associated with it. Those born in the 1940s and 1950s understood the capitalist world from the novels of Balzac, Dickens, and Victor Hugo, as well as from the writings of Marx and others. For two generations, capitalist society was regarded as an evil abyss. Marx's mention of capitalists earning 300% profits made students in classrooms shiver in fear. A deeper reason for this was that after the Communist regime assumed power in China in 1949, the country broke off relations with Western countries. Political, economic, and cultural influences came from the Soviet Union, but later Mao Zedong made the decision to cut off even these resources coming from the Soviet Union. In the 1960s, Liu Shaoqi and Deng Xiaoping tried to experiment with some capitalist economic ideas, but after 1966 those in authority alleged to be "taking the capitalist road" were overthrown and lost political power. Therefore, the "market" naturally became a pejorative political and ideological term. In the Cultural Revolution period, a classic political slogan maintained that "the weeds of socialism are preferable to the shoots of capitalism!" The basic meaning of the slogan was that in socialist China, no trace of capitalism was allowed to survive. In 1992, however, Deng Xiaoping, in his grip on the Party's power, wanted those who doubted that the "market" was appropriate for China to keep quiet and not dispute the case; this gave "the market" legitimacy and anyone could use the market to achieve their goals. Thus, ideological control was again undermined. The artists in the official artists' associations who had no opportunities to organize exhibitions now had the concept of a fantasy market, even though none of these people knew anything at all about the art market, but they were gradually learning that the market was the only thing that would allow them and their art to survive. After 1990, this was the basic context faced by Chinese artists.

With a somewhat absurd idealism, fourteen critics formed a committee of review for what would be called the Guangzhou Biennale to be held in October 1992 in the Central Hotel in Guangzhou. At the opening ceremony in the grand hall of the hotel, to the accompaniment of music by Mozart, the award-winning artists took their place on the podium. Each of the artists was asked to give a short speech and Shang Yang had this to say: "One history ends, and another begins."

However, after the Biennale's academic seminar was held in South China Botanical Gardens in Guangzhou, critic Li Xianting responded to Shang Yang's declaration by asking: Since the history of the past is unending, how can a new history begin? Li

Xianting was, of course, commenting on the country's political system, and at a time when there had been no fundamental change in the political system, people could not talk of the end of an era, let alone of a new historical beginning. As Li Xianting saw it at the time, blind market-building could not overturn the political rules of the past, which could basically only be achieved by overturning the old ideology and political system. Only this time, the threat from the art market had begun, although people like Li Xianting were saddened by this.[13]

The Guangzhou Biennale's official title evoked the name of the Guangzhou Fair, so people could see that the Biennale referred to exhibition business; the organizers strategically only included oil painting in the unwieldy official name of the Biennale, but mixed media works could later be included. However, those critics involved in the organization and curatorial work of the Biennale were well aware that this was an attempt to take advantage of a loophole in the system and that new art could hopefully break new ground and develop. To demonstrate the goals of the Guangzhou Biennale, an article titled "Moving towards the Market" provided a description of the exhibition:

> History focused on the development of metaphysical art is coming to an end. In other words, the art of China in the 1990s will comprehensively move towards the market.

There is no doubt that the essence of art's move to the market is seeking financial support. Such claims will be ethically condemned, but money in itself does not in fact have any a priori moral character or colour and it has from the beginning been subject to morality defined by different sectors of society. Today, the view that money is the source of all evil should give way to the view money forms the basic premise for awareness of the development of contemporary culture. The market in which money circulates is not a vat of corrosive culture and art, but rather a cultural production machine. In contemporary society, if an artwork is separated from gallery business, the practical actions of agents and brokers, the sound of the gavel in auction houses, and the operations of the financial banking system, not to mention the publishers, legal bodies, insurance agencies, industrial and commercial tax agencies who provide direct or indirect support, then any "success" that might accrue to it would be incredible. Once an artwork is regarded as an independent "entity" and then entrusted to society in the hope that society will affirm it, the abstract "entity" no longer exists, unless it is "actualized" through the operations of various social

> roles based on certain rules. The lubricants that constitute market mechanisms are manifested in monetary form.[14]

At the time, very few people cared for such statements and their aggressive tenor, which was in stark contrast to the concern many artists had about the marketplace.[15]

In fact, the Guangzhou Biennale created a number of problems that long prompted criticism: award-winning artists did not receive their prizes, many artists' works were not returned to them, and there was the commercial flavour of the exhibition itself. For several years, many of the artists who participated in the Guangzhou Biennale refrained from including their participation in the Biennale in their resumes, and only later when the art market was booming and the relationship between art and the market was no longer a problem did artists begin to cite their participation in this event. In any case, within the system the Guangzhou Biennale used market forces to open up a new space, and people saw it as a foretaste of future structures to be put in place; it was the efforts of the critics who participated in the Biennale that meant this exhibition provided an example for later exhibitions. The Preamble of the Biennale stated:

> The Biennale is different from any exhibition that has been held on the Chinese mainland. In the economic background of its operations, "investment" replaced the

> "sponsorship" of the past; in the subject of its operations, the company replaced the cultural institutions of the past; in operational procedures, the legally- binding contract replaced the administrative "notice" of the past; in the academic background of its operations, the evaluation committee composed of critics replaced the "selection team" of the past that had relied mainly on artists; in operational aims, the "overall effectiveness" of the economic, social, and academic spheres replaced the unitary, narrow and endless struggle for "artistic success". These characteristics of the Biennale make it clear that Chinese art history in the 1990s had really begun.[16]

In any case, the rules of the game in the 1990s really came from the West, and the vast majority of contemporary artists had great hopes of participating in international exhibitions. After Chang Tsong-Zung of Hong Kong's Hanart TZ Gallery staged *Post-89 New Art from China* in 1993, and Achille Bonito Oliva staged *Passage to the Orient* at the 45th Venice Biennale, Chinese contemporary art entered the international arena because of the "market" and other channels and a new artistic environment began.[17]

When the contemporary art market began in the 1990s, the Guardian Auction Company held the first auction of contemporary art works in 1993. However, the Chinese contemporary art market performed spectacularly beginning in 2004 and continuing until 2008 until the global financial crisis, and art followers around the world were shocked at the prices Chinese contemporary art fetched at auction houses. But in the 1980s, the modernist and contemporary artists whose concepts, ideas, styles, skills, interests, and psychology were at odds with official art standards never had a chance, given the double pressures of politics and ideology. Now, regardless of whether the market in future brings possibilities or poor results, Chinese art must negotiate the market passage, even if it leads to heaven or hell.

Notes

1. See: Central Documentation Publishing House ed., *Chronicle of Deng Xiaoping*, 2004, pp. 1272-1273.

2. See: Central Documentation Publishing House ed., *Chronicle of Deng Xiaoping*, 2004, p. 1343.

3. Of the Four Cardinal Principles, the key principle is upholding the leadership of the Party.

4. *Art·Market*, 1992:6.

5. *Art·Market*, 1992:6.

6. After the Biennale was announced, a review was conducted by the Cultural Bureau. The leadership of the Bureau (a Deputy-Director) and two subordinates viewed the works to be exhibited, and finally determined that works by eight artists could not be exhibited, including Wang Guangyi's *Great Criticism: Marlboro*. In fact, as far as I know, from 1949 onwards, no Chinese enterprise had ever invested in an art exhibition. There was no provision for this in the national art system and it was also in conflict with the ideological criteria of the government institutions that controlled art. The Guangzhou Biennale was therefore not a national exhibition staged by the government's cultural and art institutions. This was a big problem that concerned me, and even though the

Western Sichuan Company (Xi Shu Gongsi) had submitted exhibition application files, the Biennale could not be compared with the system governing exhibitions up to that point in time, so where did this exhibition find its legitimacy? Yet, in the context of the market economy and by virtue of introductions from people with whom I was familiar, the exhibition's organizing committee received a simple approval from the Bureau., This did not mean, however, that the government authorities would not inspect the contents of the exhibition. The question now was to provide the eight banned artists with the opportunity to exhibit, not to mention awarding Wang Guangyi's work first prize. I said at the Biennale that these artists' works may be cancelled, however the sponsors should return the CNY 300 application fee to the artists. The head of the Western Sichuan Company Luo Haiquan said that corporate practice was that such money was generally not returned, as is normally stipulated by contract. If the Cultural Bureau did not allow these works to be exhibited, the question was whether the Bureau could be invited to address the issue of returning the participation fee to the artists. This logic did not make any sense, of course, but at a time when all of society was becoming increasingly familiar with the market, people sometimes started thinking about and dealing with problems in accordance with market logic rather than ideological criteria. The Bureau's leadership apparently was not prepared, nor did it know how to implement its decisions, and the standards for inspecting arts were not clear-cut so when they could only rely on themselves to address the specific situation, they did not adhere to standard ideological practice. In short, I can't remember their final comments, but no one wanted to refund the application fee of the artists (which came to CNY 2,400) and eventually everything petered out into nothing, and all eight pieces went on display. Ref: Lü Peng, *Remembering the Early Nineties*, unpublished.

7. *Art·Market*, 1992:6.

8. *Art·Market*, 1991:1.

9. *Art·Market*, 1991:2.

10. *Art·Market*, 1991:3.

11. *Art·Market*, 1991:3. However, at that time he predicted: "But when we compare the earlier and later circumstances of those artists whose work is recognized as successful, you can still find some problems. The so-called career peak when the successful work appears is often after they attract commercial interest. As soon as their prices rise or stabilize at a high level, they also lose their previous allure. It is difficult to say, in turn, that this has no relationship to money, because at the same time as money is a sign of success, it also signifies the end of an artist's artistic life, or at the very least, the end of a golden age." The truth

of this statement was demonstrated by later events. An important period for Chinese contemporary art was the 1990s and the earlier experimental period of 1980s. After the year 2000, and especially after the 2004 art price "blowout", a whole group of artists ended their golden age.

12. *Art·Market*, 1992:8.

13. I described this phenomenon in a memoir:

> In fact, I would like to stress that the core problem was establishing the market system. The Guangzhou Biennale was simply the beginning of critics attempting to establish a system of art. However, people had just woken from a political nightmare, and given the many years in which an ideological judgment regarding money and markets was in place (Socialist countries had to reject the consciousness of the bourgeoisie and the capitalist system) and there was an incomplete understanding of the history of art, linking art and money made many people nervous. On 26 October, according to Shang Yang, Li Xianting has expressed a different view at the conference at the South China Botanical Gardens Pavilion in Guangzhou, history has not changed and it is what it always was. He was of course referring to the political system. I also par-

ticipated in the discussion that afternoon. I knew that the artists and critics who came to Guangzhou from other parts of China wanted to understand and discuss the Guangzhou Biennale before it opened and this created a lot of problems. Fan Di'an, for example, said: "This biennial exhibition is ultimately backed by a company that aims to make a profit. The participation of critics cannot be regarded as genuine participation, because the critics are actually employees of the company." (See: *Jiangsu Art Monthly*, 1993:2) In this regard, I was hoping to take the opportunity provided by the conference to explain the issues one by one. I pointed out that at the Guangzhou Biennale there was no connection between the business investment or business purposes and the academic accreditation committee, to ensure that critics participating in the committee remained independent; at this time I referred in particular to how the relationship between the "market" and money was not simply an economic issue, but a problem of that particular time and was even a cultural issue. On that day, the most memorable statement was that of Li Xianting. He was of the view that the Guangzhou Biennale and the Documentation Exhibition that Wang Lin was at the same time planning at the Guangzhou Academy were both examples of malignant idealism. He said that Lü Peng sitting to his right had already "fallen into the trap of business", while Wang Lin sitting on his left "is too pessimistic, and wants to shut himself off. Before I came to Guangzhou I was enthusiastic but now I'm here I'm very disappointed and very concerned that modern art is being overwhelmed by business." At this point Li Xianting stopped and people in the vicinity could clearly see that his eyes were filled with tears, and all those attending the meeting were alarmed. (Lü Peng, *Remembering the Early Nineties*, unpublished).

14. *Jiangsu Art Monthly*, 1992:10; *Art·Market*, 1992:8.

15. After this article appeared in *Jiangsu Art Monthly*, the magazine received more than one hundred letters from readers criticizing it.

16. *Art·Market*, 1992:8.

17. From 1989 to June 1993, Chinese artists and critics participated in a number of international exhibitions: in 1989 Fei Dawei curated a show in Pourrières, France titled *Chine Demain pour Hier* and worked with Jean-Hubert Martin on the *Magiciens*

de la Terre exhibition in Paris; in 1991 Leo Ou-Fan Lee and Zheng Shengtian collaborated on a show in New York titled *I Don't Want to Play Cards with Cezanne and Other Works: Selections from the Chinese New Wave and Avant-Garde Art of The Eighties*; in 1992 HanArt Gallery helped curate Chinese works at Kassel Documenta and Kong Chang'an helped curate *Cocart Bevete Arte Contemporarea* in Milan, Italy; at the beginning of 1993, Shi Andi helped curate *China Avant-garde* in Berlin, while Li Xianting and Johnson Chang co-curated *Post-89 New Art China* in Hong Kong and *Mao Goes Pop* in Sydney, Australia.

Discarding Essentialist Art

Between 1989 and 1992 most modern artists were depressed, anxious, and confused. Some critics and artists went abroad to Europe or the United States to seek new possibilities at this time, and they were the envy of most artists and critics.[1] In October 1989, Zhang Xiaogang discussed in a letter to Yang Qian in the United States the works he completed during the holidays in Kunming, and in the letter he reveals his heightened anxiety about reality: the floods in Sichuan, the heat wave in Chongqing, the earthquake in Aba, the food shortage, the rise in train fares, the sharing out of public debt, the pollution in Huangjueping, the schoolchildren dying because of pollution, and so on.

He told Yang that young teachers are talking about leaving the school, but he was conflicted about making the same choice: "If I stay here, life is already very hard, so I should go abroad. We are becoming increasingly aware of the fate and status of Chinese artists."[2] Although Yang Qian in his reply tried to persuade Zhang that it was best to go abroad because in his view the situation in China was terrible,[3] ultimately he did not convince Zhang to go to the United States. In December, in a letter to Mao Xuhui, Zhang wrote:

> A Chinese artist can only be successful abroad if he is inseparable from the background of China's current reality. Of

> course, in the special context of today, there are people who eat buns soaked in human blood. Such a person wears a Zhongshan suit and swaggers about in the presence of foreigners, declaring himself to be a "dissident".

I received a letter from Yang who advised me to go abroad, and I'm now going to write and tell him what I really think about the idea. I think this is just not the time to flee. I don't want to join Asia's "Gypsy Army". If I leave China, there will be no "art" to speak of; as long as I can paint what I want to paint, I will still stay here.[4]

In any case, at that time going abroad was an elusive thing for most people, and coping with life on a daily basis was difficult enough. This reality led people to focus on their daily lives, rather than consult books by Nietzsche and Sartre. Their ideals were clipped by their post-1989 state of shock.

In January 1990, the Tàpies exhibition was staged in Beijing and Tàpies's technique of using different materials on canvas inspired a small group of young Chinese artists who wished to continue to wrestle with the grand soul and inner tragedy to enhance textures in their work. However, this art still weighed people down and the pressure it expressed was unbearable. As a result, a group of young art teachers from Beijing's Central Academy of Arts, influenced by the historical environment in which the people of

Beijing found themselves, began to paint works on lighter themes drawn from daily life. In 1991, exhibitions were staged in Beijing of oil paintings by Liu Xiaodong (May), works by Xu Bing (May), paintings by female painters (May), oil paintings by Yu Hong, New Generation Art (July), paintings by Zhao Bandi and Li Tianyuan (September), and paintings by Shen Ling (September). These exhibitions demonstrated the artists' temperaments and styles, but they all had one common feature: themes of daily life and "proximity" (*jinjuli*), to use Yin Jinan's term. Among them, the *New Generation Art Exhibition* represented a symbolic generalization of such phenomena; many artists who took part in the exhibition indeed belonged to the New Generation, and they expressed a psychological abandonment of questions of essentialism.

In the same way as the modernist artists of the 1980s sought inspiration in European Impressionism, Fauvism, Expressionism and Surrealism, the Beijing artists of this period were responding to hyperrealism (Wei Rong) and Lucien Freud (Liu Xiaodong). Although Liu Xiaodong later stated that his art was far removed from that of Lucien Freud, he retained a memory of that artist's work. In the same way, the South-western artists such as Mao Xuhui were fond of the art of Edvard Munch. From the early 1980s onwards, young Chinese artists saw many Western art exhibitions and albums of Western art also constantly increased in number over time, which meant that their understanding of Western art was more integrated and no longer simplistic and random; they were always able to find something of the inner self in Western art, they were fond of positioning themselves within languages related to reality, and could naturally convert these to their own styles of artistic expression.

The term "New Generation" was of course the title of the exhibition, but the term also summed up the changes in the period from 1989 to 1992: the shift from the modernism of the 1980s and distancing themselves from the moods of modernism. For example, works by leading artists in Beijing in the 1980s such as Chen Wenji, Ma Lu, Cao Li and Su Xinping left people tired, and the "art institute high school generation" of Yu Hong and Wang Hao abandoned their heaviness and complexity. No one understood for sure why Wang Hao used photographic language to depict Beijing street scenes, nor did anyone understand the poses and gestures in Yu Hong's paintings of young women, but in these artists' works one could not detect suppressed desires, passionate anger, or idealistic yearning.

Could this be because these artists had discarded the heaviness of modernism and because they did not have the understanding and feeling of reality common to artists born in the 1950s that these artists were able to break out, or were they motivated by some other concept? The explanation for this phenomenon is multifaceted. In July 1991 the Museum of Chinese History staged the *New Generation Art Exhibition*;

artists included Wang Hao, Wang Huaxiang, Wang Yuping, Wang Youshen, Wang Hu, Liu Qinghe, Zhou Jirong, Wang Jinsong, Song Yonghong, Zhu Jia, Pang Lei, Yu Hong, Wei Rong, Shen Ling, Chen Shuxia, and Zhan Wang. Because of the affiliation of the sponsors, Wang Youshen, an artist working for *Beijing Youth Daily*, became one of the de facto curators. Other curators were Zhou Yan, Fan Di'an, Kong Chang'an, and Yin Jinan. The exhibition committee explained: "The exhibition is a concentrated reflection of important aspects of the present history of art, and this may be one of the most important art exhibitions in recent years, because it brings together the mentality of the times". However, in theory, summing up the New Generation was problematic; the artists did not issue their own declaration and the artists themselves said that their goal was to paint "authentic" pictures. No one understood what authentic paintings were. This provided a target for critics, who said that the "New Generation" of painters had abandoned the purpose and criticality of art and were simply a variation of the academic style, although Yi Ying, a fine arts professor from the Central Academy of Fine Arts defended the "neo-academic" style.[5] There were also critics who said that the "New Generation" was a softer generation who had retreated in the face of political trends, distancing themselves from conflicts and problems.

The critic Yin Jinan, who withdrew from working on the exhibition in midstream, had this to say:

> At present, among the few theoretical attempts to provide an explanation, there are ambiguous or unique explanations. Some have described the central idea of the New Generation or the "proximity" artists as "ridicule and self-mockery", and they have also been described as having a "punkish attitude" (*popi yishi*). Basically, the above interpretations provide the concepts of the New Generation or the "proximity" artists with a psychological position....The New Generation and the "proximity" artists were simply a new beginning, as were the 1990s. The New Generation artists tried to combine a formulaic or stylized art language with their immersion in what they felt to be proximity to real life at the outset of their art practice. Some of their works already commented on culture. The significance of the New Generation and the "proximity" artists, like all theory, had to stand the dispassionate test of history.[6]

Critics used a number of concepts and terms to summarize the art phenomenon of the early 1990s: Lü Peng wrote that "due to their background knowledge, they had no burden of history or sentimental memories"; the New Generation artists had no interest in "humanity", "ultimate goals", "the grand soul" and "salvation" that concerned artists in the 1980s.

Lü Peng describes the features of those changes:

> Concepts and mental states had changed in the face of reality, shifting from mankind to the individual, from metaphysical paradise to daily life, from the abstract to the concrete, from enthusiasm to cold detachment, from concern with saving mankind to floating freely, from analytical reason to reflective perception, from indirect imagination to direct expression, from risk-taking to placid quietude, from poetry to prose, from collectivism to individualism, from the centre to the periphery, from anxiety to indifference, from serious to flip, from responsibility to rejection, from remote to "close-up". It was because of such changes the realist works of the artists of the New Generation were so distinctly different from the "classical style" paintings of the time or the realist Scar paintings of a decade earlier.[7]

Political pressure and educational experience allowed artists almost instinctively to change direction. The phenomenon of the New Generation showed that, at the same time as they sought advantages and avoided disadvantages and retained their tastes and interests, they avoided social conflict and anything that caused psychological harm. This allowed younger artists to steer clear of the path of criticality of the previous generation. They preferred to acknowledge their own feelings and regarded the artistic purpose of their own style of painting. Their purpose could not be compared in the slightest to the critique and cultural values of earlier activists. The history of art seems to demonstrate that, like the differences that set those artists who took part in the First and Second World Wars apart from those who avoided war, those artists who regarded art as a political weapon and a tool were also great artists; in the history of 20th century Chinese art, there is no shortage of such artists.

Psychologically different from the New Generation in their use of true nature and reality as artistic themes were those artists that the critic Li Xianting described as “Cynical Realists”. The main artists exemplifying this trend were Fang Lijun and Liu Wei, and then Yue Minjun in the mid-1990s. In temperament, critics and art historians also included other artists from various cities among the group deemed to not have the earlier seriousness of purpose nor a sense of social or political resistance: Zeng Fanzhi (Beijing), Wang Jinsong (Beijing), Song Yonghong (Beijing), Deng Jianjin (Guangzhou), Zeng Hao (Guangzhou), Zhong Biao (Chongqing), Xin Haizhou (Chongqing), the brothers Guo Wei and Guo Jin (Chengdu and Chongqing), and Shen Xiaotong (Chengdu). Fang Lijun described how he denied all values or would, at least, not affirm any particular set of values. This attitude was very similar to that of characters in Wang Shuo’s novels, who were mocking, not serious, without values, and who also avoided conflict whenever possible.

In April 1992, in a museum in a converted temple on the outskirts of Beijing, Liu Wei and Fang Lijun held an exhibition of oil paintings. In the introduction to the small catalogue, Li Xianting wrote:

> I call the neo-realist trend that appeared in 1988-1989 mainly focused in Beijing "Cynical Realism" (*wanshi xianshizhuyi*). The Chinese term "*wanshi*" is almost synonymous with the English word "cynical", but it lacks the taunting cold ridicule of the English term's cool detachment from reality and life. However, Cynical Realism represented a new cultural tendency in the modernist ideological trend of the 1980s. The 1989 *China/Avant-Garde: China Modern Art Exhibition* marked the end of a phase of China's new wave art of the 1980s, and at the same time it represented a heavy blow to the idealistic attempt to introduce Western modern culture to rescue and reconstruct China's new culture. Cynical Realism was the inevitable spiritual product in the face of a shattered psychological state.[8]

Cynical Realism art was regarded by some critics as philistinism in its rejection of the critical stance of the 1980s but, in analysing the phenomenon, Li Xianting regarded it as a special form of resistance. He saw the "sense of ennui" expressed by these artists in the following way:

> Their sense of ennui led them to abandon earlier art's idealism and heroics and the promethean heights from which the previous two generations of artists viewed man, and to switch to a mundane view of their position in reality. Their ennui spelled pointlessness and their pointlessness meant that they did not have to show respect, and so their ennui also prompted them to laugh at themselves, and to be irreverent, cynical, and indifferent in attitude when describing themselves and the familiar, boring, incidental and absurd lives that surrounded them, which shaped the artistic style of their hooligan (*popi*) humour.[9]

The values of Cynical Realism were ambiguous, but its attitude was far removed from the obligatory official political position. In language, Cynical Realism retained images, but the artist could consciously debase these images, and make full use of modified designs and ready-made images to create his own repertoire of images. In the work of these artists, one could sense aspects of the Chinese temperament: self-deprecation (and self-abasement), exaggeration, a lack of realism, opportunism, refusal to adopt a position, smugness, and helplessness. Fang Lijun included schematic images of his friends and himself in his works, Liu Wei relied on photographs of his parents, and Yue Minjun included designs based on his own grinning face; such paintings were completely different from the visually imitative objects and the thinking in the paintings of the New Generation artists.

At about the same time, pop art related to society, politics, and history emerged. Initially, the Wuhan artists regarded the emergence of commercial society as providing the raison d'être for their pop art. The tight controls exerted by politics and ideology had quickly driven people into business, and during this period, a large number of publications appeared discussing the phenomenon; many people in Party and government organs, state enterprises and institutions made the strategic decision to leave their jobs and take up work in a commercial company or set up their own business. In a book on current affairs published in 1992 titled *China's Big Bang Theory* (People's China Publishing House) a number of slogans appeared on the title page: "the sleeping lion of the Orient is woken up by money"; "the political challenge of stocks and shares"; "the market controls China"; and "law and the economy advance together".

Another work of reportage and research titled *Chinese Intellectual Upheaval* had the subtitle: "Chinese Intellectuals Cast Anchor in the Stormy Sea of Business". According to the logic of traditional Chinese thinking, businessmen are lower-level people in society, because of their alleged venality, lack of education, and retrograde thought. Yet this book revealed how during this period a large number of famous intellectuals in China had gone into business and a section of the book discussing the phenomenon was titled: "Elegy for China's Contemporary Literati: The Choice Mammon or the Muses".

In spring 1992 advertisements for the Guangzhou Biennale, the first large-scale exhibition of the modernist art movement (soon to be called "contemporary art") in China since 1989 appeared, and these did not shy away from the market question which stimulated the enthusiasm of many young artists. Initially, the Guangzhou Biennale was where the pop art trend of Wuhan was first exhibited, and in 1993 pop art emerged as part of the "Post-89 New Art" in Shanghai and Beijing. Li Xianting used the term "Political Pop" to describe that art and its zeitgeist:

> Most Political Pop artists were born in the 1950s, which meant that they were influenced by a particular historical context and familiar with the Cultural Revolution; they understood its political background and had even experienced many historical events. The question for them now was how to bid farewell to or critique this past history.

Artist Yu Youhan explained in July 1997:

> I paint Mao Zedong, generally speaking, to depict China, her history, and my own experience of life. However, as an artist, this expression is what I like and what I am able to do. The period of Deng Xiaoping's reform and opening has provided Chinese artists

with more room for their activities and this has enabled me to depict Mao Zedong, the most famous person in modern China, in my own style of artistic expression. My childhood and youth were in the Mao era, and I experienced the Cultural Revolution. In the Cultural Revolution period, there were photographic portraits of Mao Zedong everywhere in China. More than ten years later, when I recreate these photos, I believe art is a meaningful thing. I spontaneously think of a bust of Mao Zedong on Tiananmen, his monochromatic uniform printed with designs, and when I look at this picture, I feel happier than ever. The painting expresses ideas I have stored in my heart for more than 10 years but was never sure I could articulate. I think it is interesting that this painting contains a contrast between two eras: the contents of the Mao era, and the treatment of the era of reform and opening up.

In the art of Political Pop, the most familiar works are Wang Guangyi's *Great Criticism* series. Wang Guangyi's works concisely presented the two ideologies coexisting in China, as described by He Qingji in his "China's New Art Post-89":

> Political Pop is the interesting mix of socialism and capitalism, and I believe it is related to the rapid development of consumerist

> culture in recent years in China. It is interesting that Political Pop from time to time uses images of the Cultural Revolution period, and the "red, bright, and light" visual decoration. Political pop can conceal mockery, but the strength of its targeting and critique is difficult to ascertain.

The images in Great Criticism constructed from "workers, peasants and soldiers", ubiquitous in the earlier Cultural Revolution period posters, were now placed in ambiguous juxtapositions of images used to attack the bourgeoisie and capitalist commodity advertising, thus providing people with schemata to freely interpret questions of reality. The unique style of such art was intended to be vastly different from the thematic modernism of the 1980s, and also to be fundamentally different from earlier paintings that used visual objects to form their language. Artists were no longer dependent on nature and objectivity, and they could directly appropriate and transform earlier cultural products to form their own artworks. This was an obvious extension of the art of Richard Hamilton and Andy Warhol. At the same time, the confusion implicit in the discussion on the purification of art language in the late 1980s was cleared up by such concepts of art, as for example by Li Shan's use of photographs of Mao Zedong in his early years, though Li Shan eliminated Mao's historical significance by applying makeup to his image. The artist's image did not come from any image seen and relied exclusively on his selection and cropping of existing images to use in accordance with his own artistic views. Taking into account the dissemination in the early 1990s of Derrida's deconstruction in Chinese academic circles, avant-garde circles in Hubei Province also liked to engage with his ideas, and we can also see these art concepts as stemming from the influence of post-modern philosophy..

The editor of *Jiangsu Art Monthly* Gu Chengfeng wrote, when analysing the background against which China Pop Art was produced:

> Various media have increased the pace of change to an unprecedented extent, and the visual images produced by television, electronic games, copiers, faxes, advertising, karaoke, and beauty pageants have already transcended the scope of entertainment and consumption to impact deeply on a generation's lifestyle and mode of thinking; culture is a fashion which is instantaneous, consumer-based, and superficial. Such a fashion not only constantly challenges orthodox culture, but demands to be expressed in the art of the day. This is the unique environment that produced Chinese Pop Art. This specific environment translated the concepts of rapidity, immediacy, fame, popularity, and effect into the domain of art. In this sense Chinese Pop Art corresponded to how Richard Hamilton

> casually described Pop Art in the 1950s: "popular, transient, expendable, low-cost, mass-produced, young, witty, sexy, gimmicky, glamorous, and Big Business".[10]

As an art strategy, Political Pop can be regarded as one way in which the modernist art of the 1980s ultimately transformed into a mainstream ideological trend as "contemporary art". The political conflict and ideological challenge reflected in Political Pop works were strengthened as each side in the conflict perpetuated the strategic East-West confrontations in politics, culture and economics, and so extended its meaning. The presence of this logic and the political and ideological colouring of the artworks were relied upon by many Chinese avant-garde artists and critics as the point of departure and goal in marketing avant-garde art and this saw Political Pop flourish within a very short span of time.

As a stratagem of opposition to the political system in the 1990s, Political Pop was almost one of the few remaining stances of opposition to absolutism. However, it did not provoke any strong counterattack, and the centre of political power in China never adopted any effective opposition to the attitudes of Political Pop. As party to the overall ideology, the authorities in the Chinese art world could only issue boring statements,[11] and were unable to initiate any sustained political movement as they had done in the past. This demonstrates that there was a noticeable change at this time in the discourse and system of authority in ideological and "political" debate. As the result of the introduction of a number of forces and of the increasing complexity of power structures (with elements that were domestic and international, political and economic, cultural and ideological, individual and collective, mental and physical), the intrinsically absolutist attitudes of both sides reached a de facto compromise in the context of the legitimization of the market.

Indeed, around 1992, there were tangible political compromises and changes at the centre of state power, and the major issue in the political life of the country was no longer whether social reform was necessary, but rather how reform could be carried out and who would hold the power to reform. This time people began to sense the vacuum created by the collapse in prices and the embarrassment of the disappearance of truth. In such a scenario, the narrative for the ambitious goals may be a vague shout or ridiculous struggle.

The art languages of Political Pop and American Pop art were more or less similar. However, unlike works by Hamilton, Warhol, and Lichtenstein, the works by Chinese artists were more metaphorical and suggestive. In fact, the political significance of these pop art works was strengthened by ideological conflict. In *China Times* (18 March 1993), an article titled "Speaking for Chinese Pop" hit out at Political Pop with ideology: "After 1989, artists in several places borrowed the corpse of Western Pop art to criticize or ridicule the soul of politics"; the artist speaking to the journalist in this interview was being doubly ironic in so describing the politics and consumerism he treated in his own Pop Art works.[12] For Chinese avant-garde artists and critics, the additional ideology undoubtedly had immediate benefits: by enhancing the "political" meaning, Pop Art works targeted ideology. The term "Political Pop" could be interpreted to mean "the politicization of pop art."

Cynical Realism and Political Pop made use of the background provided by the market economy to extend the reach of ideological management; given that there were no slogans or effective political terms, any method of metaphor, allusion, symbol, restructuring, appropriation, or bricolage could constitute a tool to be freely used by the artist. By about 1995, the styles of Cynical Realism and the "Gaudy Art" that perpetuated it and was even closer to consumer society, merged. Throughout the 1990s, Chinese contemporary art was gradually beginning to be collected by Western museums and acquiring greater space in galleries, which provided conditions for contemporary art facing reduced opposition in China. In other words, official management structures in China lost control over art: the market classified everything as a commodity and even ideology was a commodity that could be traded freely. This social and political environment provided conditions for richer artistic practice, including performance art,

art installations, audio-visual art, and mixed media. After the mid-90s, Chinese contemporary art continued to spread under the influence of every form of Western art. Especially after 1993, artists could see any shows they wished in foreign art museums, from classical and modern art to contemporary art, from Rembrandt, Vermeer, Monet, Kandinsky, and Picasso to Jeff Koons, Matthew Barney, Damien Hirst, Anselm Keifer and Gerhard Richter.

Notes

1. Critics Gao Minglu and Zhou Yan, as well as the artist Xu Bing, went to the United States, while critics Fei Dawei and Hou Hanru and the artist Huang Yongping went to France.

2. "Letter to Yang Qian from Zhang Xiaogang (6 October)", in Zhang Xiaogang, Lü Peng ed., *Amnesia and Memory: Zhang Xiaogang's Correspondence, 1981-1996*, Peking University Press, 2010, pp. 138-140.

3. Yang Qian replied sympathetically in a letter of 25 November: "I completely understand your situation. Here we all know about what is happening in China, but it's not appropriate to talk about it here. The only solution I can see is that you leave. Wait until things improve next year. Maybe you could get to the West through the Spanish Embassy, and then come on to the US? After I get my green card, I will do whatever I can to help you. It seems like everyone in China is clamouring to go abroad, so getting a visa will be even harder in the future, so you will need to find a way." "Letter from Yang Qian to Zhang Xiaogang (25 November)", in Zhang Xiaogang, Lü Peng ed., *Amnesia and Memory: Zhang Xiaogang's Correspondence, 1981-1996*, Peking University Press, 2010, p. 140.

4. "Letter to Mao Xuhui from Zhang Xiaogang (18 December)", in Zhang Xiaogang, Lü Peng ed., *Amnesia*

and Memory: Zhang Xiaogang's Correspondence, 1981-1996, Peking University Press, 2010, pp. 144-145.

5. Yi Ying discussed this phenomenon:

> Unlike the Western modernism that completely wiped out the traditional academy system, Chinese new wave art was not in serious opposition to the system of college education that was in place, even though new wave art was something that did not fit into these art schools. It is interesting that many students of the Academy of Fine Arts could happily reconcile painting boring orthodox figures in their painting classes while busying themselves with modernist experiments outside school. There was a complex background to this phenomenon. It can be stated overall that on the one hand classes would cater to classicism, while on the other modernism came with a sense of urgency which in addition to social needs and market trends provided room for the survival of traditional skills of realism in Chinese colleges. This cannot be simply explained as a diversification of art styles, regardless of which it can be said that such a background created the conditions for the emergence and development of the neo-academic school of painting. The neo-academic school of painting that

emerged within campus culture encompassed two layers of meaning: first, traditional academic techniques (regardless of whether they were Soviet-style or European-style) played a role in and influenced students' acceptance of modern culture; second, given China's specific historical conditions, art college became a centre of information about modernism and concepts of Western modern art were studied and absorbed in this environment, as well as being gradually integrated into the art language of some young faculty members and their students. This second aspect of meaning was more significant. (*Art Research*, 1990:4, p. 19.)

6. *Jiangsu Art Monthly*, 1992:1, p. 17.

7. Lü Peng, *A History of Art in Twentieth-Century China*, Paris: Somogy, 2013, p. 599.

8. The term "cynical realism" first appeared in Li Xianting's August 1991 essay entitled "The Sense of Ennui and the Third Generation of Artists Since the Cultural Revolution". In early 1993, the inaugural issue of *Genesis* presented a column by Dao Zi titled "Café Guerbois", which carried an article completed by Li Xianting in early 1992 entitled "Post-Modern Tendencies in Chinese Art Circles since 1989". To this article Li Xianting appended a footnote more fully

explaining "Cynical Realism" and its historical and cultural connections with the concepts of "punkish humour" and "hooligan culture".

9. *Genesis*, no. 1, 1993, p. 44.

10. Gu Chengfeng, "Chinese Pop Trends", Chinese Art in the 1990s, 1990-1992, Urumqi: Xinjiang Fine Arts and Photography Press, p. 92.

11. In February 1997, *Art Newsletter*, the organ of the China Artists Association, published a speech by the painter Li Qi, renowned for having once painted Mao Zedong and later Chinese leaders, at the China Artists Association's forum for learning from the spirit of the Chinese Communist Party plenum. This "authoritative figure", who had lost his influence in the art world, attacked Political Pop in a speech entitled "Open Your Eyes" and described how the problems created by this artistic phenomenon threatened the nation's "spiritual civilization". In his speech, Li Qi noted that "there were many Political Pop works in the *Third National Exhibition of Chinese Oil Painting*, which was supported by no less an institution than the Arts Council of the PRC Ministry of Culture", and the "three curators of the Exhibition were no less than those officials of the Arts Council in charge of art's reputation!" (Ref: *Art Newsletter*, February 1997, pp. 3-5) The *Arts Newsletter* is the official bulletin of the art establishment, but the publication is only

circulated to association members and has virtually no influence, so Li Qi's remarks could not be disseminated effectively, unlike in the past when statements by such "authorities" would have carried weight.

12. In an interview published in the English-language journal Window on February 5, 1993, under the title "A Reflection of Changing Times" Wang Guangyi talked about his paintings and the ideas behind them during his brief stay in Hong Kong in the week prior to publication:

> I used to believe in art for art's sake, but not anymore," says Wang, a tall northerner who sports a beard, something rarely seen among his fellow countrymen. "My paintings are my thoughts in picture form. Through Great Criticism, for example, I try to express my view on both the ideology of the Mao era and the current craze for Western consumer products in China. The paintings tease both. "Political or ideological movements have been so much a part of the Chinese life in the last few decades, pop art simply cannot escape it," says Wang explaining his fascination with political themes.
>
> "In fact I like Western consumer goods too," he continues, taking a puff of an Yves Saint Laurent cigarette, "but at the same time I can't help looking with a critical eye at the impact of Western pop culture upon

Chinese youth nowadays. The worker-peasant-soldier images in my art were my way of expressing the paradox. I can't say that my thoughts on this issue are crystal clear, but I feel it is the vagueness that inspires me in the first place.

The Context of the New Century

From 2008 onwards, China became embroiled in the global economic crisis, as the inevitable endpoint in a process initiated by a political decision made at the Third Plenary Session of the Eleventh Party Central Committee some 30 years previously. At that momentous gathering, the Communist Party of China (CPC) shifted its political line from one in which "class struggle" served as the "key link" to a policy stressing economic construction. This led to the gradual introduction into socialist China of the laws and regulations needed to sustain a capitalist market economy. By the first decade of the 21st century, the status of the Chinese market might not yet have been fully acknowledged by the international community, but China's accelerating participation in the process of globalization was patently obvious.

The economic crisis made Chinese artists and critics fully realize the nature of globalization's impact. Indeed, according to the usual view and experience, globalization stemmed from economic strength. Economists such as Alan Rugman define globalization as multinational firms crossing national boundaries, engaging in foreign direct investment, and setting up commercial networks to create activities of value. Other scholars think globalization should be interpreted as a process of complex change in many diverse fields including the economy, politics, culture, and technology. But it is the combined strength of politics and culture generated by economic forces that actually impacts on all other human activities in a comprehensive way. Against such a background, Chinese artists faced two difficult choices: On the one hand, they clearly realized that local criteria of value cannot provide the authority and legitimacy for artistic value judgments; on the other hand, the construction of a Chinese national culture is also subject to global pressures but China, unlike Western countries, has not gone through the process of systematically constructing a national culture, and so, in the absence of Western choices and opportunities, Chinese artists can sense a loss of the basis of their values, and when Westerners make choices it is hard to avoid the suspicion that these choices are "cultural colonialism".

In the art world, discussions in the 1990s on several artistic questions may have extended into the new century in different forms, and those artists who were important players in modernist and contemporary art in the 1980s and 1990s were now already middle-aged. Artistic sensitivity and differences about artistic issues were now the concerns of a younger generation of artists. However, investigating the work of these young Chinese artists was already different from analysing the art of artists born in the 1950s and 1960s. Most artists born in the 1970s, especially those born after the mid-seventies, have no direct experience of history before 1978. They were born once China had begun to restore the national economy and to use Western thought – especially Western liberal thought – to undertake a critical summary and analysis of the Cultural Revolution period from 1966 to the end of 1976. The young directly benefited from the opening to Western knowledge and thought and the relatively relaxed freedom of speech of that time, but could read nothing in their textbooks about the thirty years of Chinese history from 1949 to 1978. Thus, although they had acquired some new Western knowledge, they lacked the experience to make any historical comparisons. Indeed, Western thought already permeated intellectual discourse and every corner of society, but in the field of education which officialdom controlled, the political and moral education which students from primary school to university received was mainly confined to Party ideology and government propaganda. No basic knowledge about human civilization or any traditional ethical teaching was wholly or systematically imparted, and as for universal values and concepts – these were fuzzy notions from the West which China had never fully discussed, and officialdom has continued to the present day to remind the population how hostile Western forces will use these as a pretext to subvert socialist China, so if necessary, statements about universal values are often subject to critique.[1] It is true that the Party and the media at times invoke concepts of democracy, fairness and justice, but the political system of this country remains one-party rule, and "socialism" continues to exist both as an ideological concept and as a social system. Among the many ironies is that even though the intellectual emancipation of the 1980s provided the possibility for individualism of different forms and modes, this did not mean that everybody has acquired a systematic understanding of democratic systems and free thought; some young people interpret individual freedom to mean that one can do whatever one wants, and so they lack any situational or historical consciousness for discussing related concrete issues. Most of them are unaware that whatever freedom or individualism they have today is related to the adoption in July 1977 by the 10th Central Committee of the Communist Party of China at its 3rd plenary session of the "Resolution on Comrade Deng Xiaoping Resuming His Post"; they do not realize that the current situation is also related to the publication on 10 May 1978 in *Theoretical Trends*, the internal organ of the CPC's Party School, of an article authorized by Hu Yaobang (1915-1989) and titled "Practice is the Sole Criterion for Testing Truth"; they are also unaware of the connection with the 25 November 1978 decision made at the working conference of the CPC Central Committee's plenary session reversing the original verdict that those involved in the Tiananmen Incident of 5 April 1976 were "counter-revolutionaries". Few people have concerned themselves with later questions: What was ultimately the great historical significance of the decision of the Third Plenary Session of the Eleventh Party Central Committee on 18 December 1978 to make the focus of all Party work from 1979 onwards "the switch to the socialist modernization drive"? The young could only enjoy the benefits of these events, and even regarded the freedoms of today and the legitimacy of the individual's private world as natural things, not knowing the underlying background and political reasons for this "natural" situation.

Since 1949, Chinese art has been inextricably linked with politics. At the beginning of the eighties, critics called on people to pay greater attention to the aesthetic function of art, and to abandon the position that art is the tool of doctrine. Because of history – especially the ten-year history of the Cultural Revolution, to the present day artists and critics have tended to avoid the vocabulary of "politics". Unlike economists, who regard politics as a mechanism that accompanies the distribution of public goods, artists and critics mainly interpret politics as thought, concepts, and ideology, and in this way, for reasons of inertia and ideology, contemporary artists often either intentionally or unintentionally combine art with political matters, but invariably never elaborate on the relationship between art and politics. Artistic and critical circles still strenuously avoided sensitive political issues, even though political issues are constantly at the forefront of questions related to journalism, the Internet media, exhibition inspections, and the allocation of resources. At the same time, the complexity of social affairs has also led to complexity in the expression of politics – for example, political sensitivity stemming from ecological problems, from the process of appropriating and demolishing people's houses and then relocating them as an aspect of urbanization, and even from rescue efforts during natural disasters.

Just as the works of many young artists proclaim, the high-speed development of the market economy and material "progress" – mainly in the urban context – have satisfied people's basic demands, and at a time when "made in China" is also becoming a fashionable concept globally, many people – including of course those young artists – very naturally seemed to readily regard today's world as one very different from that perceived by artists born in the 1950s and 1960s. In academic and art circles, the two decades since the beginning of the 1990s brimming with 'post-modern' theory, the streets and lanes flush with goods that circulate in world markets, and the global links established by the Internet even delude people into thinking that national boundaries are illusory. In artistic circles, it had become routine for artists to fly to New York, Paris, Venice, London and numerous other cities in Western countries to participate in exhibitions or attend activities; the net effect of this also blurred the notion of borders – between nations, histories, politics, economies, cultures, ideologies and even habits and customs, and these feelings also blurred people's judgmental lines of vision.

Changes in the material world generally led people to think that the reform and market economy had basic legitimacy, based on the indirect and latent characteristics of the impact of politics on daily life and on the basis of society's lack of any new guiding values. As a result, with the development of the economy, background interests, experience and personal knowledge began to influence people's judgments. The 2000 Shanghai Biennale gave some people the feeling that ideology had been dispelled and the atmosphere was filled with globalization, because the different concepts of art, taste, and interest, as well as profit demands of the Biennale's policymakers, operators and participants, together with their varying degrees of political sensitivity, dispelled any unified ideological criteria. Many critics still doubted that the reality of such "globalization" could enjoy any assurances from the political system in China, but the political regulation of the early 1990s that the demarcation lines between "capitalism" and "socialism" could not be crossed-sustained and perpetuated this non-debatable reality by not allowing it to surface as ideological conflict. In 1999, Harald Szeeman selected nineteen Chinese artists to take part in the theme exhibition of the 48th Venice Biennale, but few in Chinese art circles noticed this was Chinese contemporary art's "grand moment" in a globalized context. Regardless, the Shanghai Biennale of 2000 was regarded as a sign that Chinese contemporary art had acquired international status and legitimacy. Later, in 2002, the Guangdong Art Museum, one of China's three major official art museums, staged the First Guangzhou Triennial of Contemporary Art entitled *Reinterpretation: A Decade of Experimental Chinese Art (1990-2000)*. The works bizarrely described as "experimental art" were regarded as representing another step towards China's legitimization of the "avant-garde", "modern art", "the new wave" and "contemporary art". At the same time, the question of the curator came to the fore with the constant stream of exhibitions and the core of the question hinged upon who determined the themes of exhibitions and who determined the direction in which exhibitions were moving. People knew that in earlier years the official artists' associations had determined the themes of exhibitions and exercised control over them. At the same time, inspired by Beijing's 798 Art District, the art districts in a number of cities (such as Shanghai's Moganshan M50, Kunming's Loft and Chengdu's Blue Roof Art District) supported curatorial work, and regardless of whether the financing for these spaces came from the market or from funding, they all became active forces in the construction of a new art system. The market also encouraged the emergence of private art galleries, and even though many of the galleries (such as the Upriver Art Museum and the Dongyu Art Museum) of the 1990s had a short-lived history, the strong market led to the appearance of the Today Art Museum in Beijing (June 2002), Zendai Art Museum in Shanghai (July 2005), Sifang Art Museum in Nanjing (August 2005), and most recently Chengdu MOMA (2011), Shanghai Long Museum (2012), and the Yu Deyao Museum (2014). All these developments are the result of changes in the new art environment.

In China, people have for a long time been forced to accept the view that economics and politics were quite separate: thus, capitalist markets and technology serve the socialist economy, and a market economy and socialism are not contradictory. However, this kind of explanation provided no corresponding foundation in the political system, nor was there any unified system of value judgments for the fields of literature and art. Some contemporary artists and critics (mainly professors in some institutes) had different degrees of contact with the political system, simply by being for example teachers or professors in institutes, and in different spaces with different degrees of intensity and technology they relied on moving back and forth, inside and outside the system. However, this did not mean that there were no demarcation lines around the political system. Since the beginning of the 1990s, two realities – the reality of the system and the one outside the system – had gradually taken shape in parallel, and regardless of however fuzzy the artistic criteria of the political system were, the old ideology and the official standards that depended on it for their survival continued to exist; the "main tune" which officialdom propagated was merely an ambiguous substitute term for what had in the past been called "political tasks". Those artists who needed to rely on galleries and the market were not controlled by such criteria in the slightest. As a result, there were two art worlds in China, even though information about these two art worlds was often presented to the world on the same website, e.g. Artron.

After the year 2000, nobody could convincingly point in which direction art would develop, and at a time when the legal identity of capitalists (who, if willing, could now also join the ranks of the Communist Party as a proletarian vanguard!) occupied the mainstream, the questions of whom art should serve and the direction in which art should develop had further emerged in the mechanism of art. The complicated economic sectors had produced complex social strata, but ultimately the question was which stratum was the main strength in this society, or did the different strata constitute a new historical totality? Within the official art system few people contemplated, or could even articulate, these questions.

Most people could see that the economic reforms seriously challenged the authority of the old system, as well as the right of "experts" and "authorities" to speak out. Wu Guanzhong was an older painter within the system, and he was an interesting special case, because he frankly stated that the Federation of Literary and Art Circles, the "artists' associations", and the state academies were necessarily suspect, and this made official "authorities" and "experts" extremely tense and enraged. Basically speaking, they found that Wu's criticism of them challenged their very legitimacy in this new historical period. In fact, these organizations continued to exist throughout the period in which the market economy rapidly developed, because there had been no change in the political system of China, and the old ideological criteria in the worlds of culture and art still existed. In step with the reforms and seeing things from the positions of tactics and cost accounting, the costs consumed by these organizations were insignificant compared with other areas of the old system; because of the system itself, the propaganda function of art still occupied an important position in the work of ideological administrative departments, and so the continuation of these organizations still had a political raison d'être, since the power of the markets and their institutional improvement had still not impinged on the power of mandatory intervention that these organizations enjoyed. At the same time, because art works had the attribute of being goods that could be immediately exchanged for currency, those people in the system who consumed taxpayers' money could similarly place their own works in the market through the use of power and skilful language; as a result, they not only had power and capital but also obtained material benefits offered by the market at the same time, and they made use of the twin opportunities presented from within the political system (power) and outside the political system (markets). From this perspective, capital also played a part in maintaining the old system.

One phenomenon which perplexed critics in the first ten years of the new century entailed the startlingly sky-high prices that Cynical Realist and Political Pop art works produced since 1993 were realizing on international markets. Until 2008, critics launched direct attacks on the artists and works that obtained such high prices in auction salesrooms. Meanwhile, also participating in this criticism of high-price artists were some critics of the older generation, such as Gao Minglu, who had lived for the previous 20 years in the U.S.A., but who clamoured to add his voice to those of these critics. On the other hand, Chinese contemporary art since the beginning of the 1990s had never received approval from the official "artists' associations", and even in December 2008, the Chinese Artists' Association's "Work Report" still singled out contemporary art for censure. As a consequence the two artistic phenomena – Cynical Realism and Political Pop – found themselves consistently the brunt of two groups of critics – those critics of high-price artists mentioned previously who had never made their values and position clear, and the official line spelled out by the "artists' associations".

Politics still functions as a brake on contemporary art by controlling the mechanisms of public property. One only has to investigate the history of the fine arts since 1979 to realize that whenever there is any discussion on the platform for artistic exchange, or on the environments in which art works are exchanged and artists receive the costs and resources from this trade, one can see the influence politics exerts on contemporary art: it is the official fine arts organizations that really hold the legal power, the opportunities, and the resources to conduct exchanges, and these official organizations control the right to represent the country and the right to distribute the relevant resources. Those contemporary Chinese artists who already play a significant role in the international community have never become the representatives of China's contemporary national culture, and it is the enforcers (or messengers) of the national ideology, the National Artists' Association, who have no understanding at all of the position in the world of these artists, but suspect instead that there is some ulterior motive behind the forces that have pushed these Chinese artists to prominent status.

However, inexplicably, on 13 November 2009, the "China Contemporary Art Academy", an affiliate of the official China Art Academy, formally opened in Beijing. The first president of the institute was Luo Zhongli, whose painting *Father* depicted a man who had endured great hardships, but Luo had managed to endure censure from those who adhered to the old ideology. Before the event, invitations to attend the inauguration and to express their congratulations had been issued to officials of important departments of the Party and state (Propaganda Department of the CPC Central Committee, Ministry of Culture, China Federation of Literary and Art Circles, and artists' associations). The president of the National Artists' Association also attended and conveyed his congratulations. At the ceremony, people realized that among the members of the new institution there were many artists, such as Wang Guangyi, Zhang Xiaogang, Yue Minjun and Fang Lijun, who could never have been acknowledged as contemporary artists by the official artists' associations. Against a background where their value had not been acknowledged, these artists now held the hands of officialdom. This was seen as "capitulation" on their part by younger artists and critics, and as the end of their critical spirit. Previously, the astonishing prices contemporary art was fetching in the art market starting in 2005 had been attracting attention, and until the outset of the economic crisis in 2008, sharp fluctuations in the market prices of contemporary art also provided the opportunity for sceptical critics to question the Chinese art market, leading to clouded judgment shrouding some contemporary art and artists.

In fact, the value of art criticism was in a confused and unclear state throughout the art world. In 2008 at a conference on Chinese contemporary art attended by Western and Chinese scholars,[2] one Western participant asked a Chinese critic to explain to him what was unique about Chinese contemporary art and its significance for world art history. The background to this question was of course the affects beyond the realm of economics of the "rise" of China. Specifically, Western scholars' attention had been directed to the constantly growing prices that Chinese art works were fetching at auction. In China, some critics regarded this phenomenon as something that had been merely cooked up by businessmen, but they could not explain why it was contemporary art rather than official art or some other type of art that attracted market attention. On many questions what was vexing was perhaps what relationship existed between Chinese contemporary art and Chinese art traditions, and there were no materials available to the Chinese conference participants to provide an informed answer. It can be imagined that given China's rapidity (this rapidity being apparent in all sectors), Chinese critics were not completely prepared for providing an answer to the question. According to the usual intellectual logic a basic critical framework should have been available, but for some time, Chinese critics had not worked to provide one and it seemed that within a very short time it had become very difficult to provide a clear basis for making judgments.

Indeed, China's economic development had led to a lot of conjecture. In 2009 when the Hollywood film *2012* was shown in China, it did well at the box office because the film addressed many of the problems mankind would have to face together in the future. Even though the film's director (who was not of course an engineer concerned by life's realities) points out the importance of "China's rapidity" for saving mankind, the complex and distorted background to "China's rapidity" is not discussed in the film. Whether or not the crisis can be resolved by mankind is a question that cannot be answered, but for real people the question before them can clearly be judged: the intrusion and intensification of social inequalities, the massive degradation of the environment, and large-scale ecological destruction are all the result of "China's rapidity". On the afternoon of 19 December,

2009 the Copenhagen Conference on Climate Change concluded in an atmosphere of wrangling and disappointment. The various participating countries in the battle to reduce their goals and responsibilities revealed the imbalance in profits and power that exists. Even though the Chinese delegates explained that there needed to be a historical view of development, China is nevertheless one of the world's major greenhouse gas-emitting nations, and the questions of reducing carbon emissions and environmental pollution are major problems for China's development. In other words, as China globalizes it needs to bravely shoulder the responsibilities of a world power and necessarily reform its original system and management system. However, daily events and existing problems show how serious and difficult their resolution is, and mass violent incidents come close to spinning out of control. At the same time, ethnic problems in Tibet and Xinjiang have never been as thorny as they are today. The daily details and information about problems arising from economic development, political reform and ethnic conflict enter the spiritual world of the artist in all their complexity, and he or she can respond consciously or unconsciously on the basis of his or her own unique knowledge, background and experience.

On December 10, 2010, when at a session of Hanhai Autumn Auctions devoted to pre-modern and modern paintings from the Qingyun Tang Collection, a work painted by Xu Beihong in 1938 and titled

Baren Jishui Tu fetched CNY 153 million (over CNY 171 million including commission), the question of the art market again became a hot topic in the media. The art market had not ground to a halt because of the earlier economic crisis or because of its criticism by the art world. On the contrary, even more capital was flowing into it, and when people heard that many private funds were entering the art auction market, this meant that capital investments had replaced the previous private collectors who bought at auction based on family inheritance, interest and knowledge. People were concerned that the large-scale influx of capital might have a detrimental effect on art production, because at that time the concept that money corrupted the soul was still widespread. Those with an ethical sense of values were unable to have sufficient faith in neutral money being rationally used. At the same time, 2010 was also regarded as the first year in which funds were injected into art exchanges within China, and investment in artworks had already evolved into an accompaniment of capital and not merely an interest or passion. However, in that year Chinese auction houses exceeded CNY 50 billion in sales (the sales in the previous year were less than half of this) and people were hopeful: the value of civilization and art had rapidly commanded attention and great respect. People could see that the Chinese art market of today had expressed respect for art through prices, an artwork being capable of representing spiritual wealth and material value at the same time, and this was a rational historical turn. However much critics might clamour about those markets, if people compared today's situation to that at the beginning of the Republic when treasures from Dunhuang were looted and sent abroad or to the days of the Cultural Revolution when the Red Guards had destroyed antiquities, then it was easy to come to this more rational historical conclusion.

Most intellectuals agreed. Capital was not a simple economic concept but a manifestation of a sense of value. China found itself in a transitional period of very rapid change, and this transformation was not simply confined to China's degree of industrialization, urbanization or GDP per capita, but more importantly to the direction in which China would move: the core question was into what type of state and society with what sense of values China would evolve. To the present day, China has not acknowledged the basic rationale of any sense of "universal values", even though China has signed the International Treaty on Human Rights, and this is because such values are an expression of Western civilization and are regarded as containing elements that will subvert socialism. In the first half of the twentieth century, science and democracy advocated by the May Fourth New Culture Movement overthrew the ideology and concepts of the Confucian order that had ruled China for a long time, but the bitter anti-Japanese struggle abruptly terminated the development of this intellectual conflict. In the 1980s people continued to draw on Western thought in the "intellectual emancipation movement" of that time that once again promoted science and democracy and delivered a critique of Stalinist and Mao Zedong authoritarianism. Yet modernization based on "economic construction" did not lead to a rejection of the old ideology (dogmatic Marxist historical materialism) and the construction of a new system (constitutional democracy). There was no civil society that could provide a basis for these ideas and system. As a result, following the growth of the economy, problems of social justice and truth became increasingly more obvious, and the gap between rich and poor rapidly widened. In the last few years, people have debated whether China needs to adopt "universal values" or can it create a "Chinese model"? Can China continue to develop the economy using nationalism while maintaining a one-party autocracy, without there being any abrupt change in the structure of state power and social management? These questions are all related to art, because they impinge on the allocation of state resources for artistic development and the legitimization of the value systems of art, as well as on whether the art world needs guarantees of its new values and system. Moreover, the true basis and content of the nation's art strategy depends on the resolution of these questions. In today's China, there has been no change in a system in which ideology is based on politics and provides the only authority for legality. In the wake of massive changes in material life this has led to correspondingly severe losses in spirituality, morality and values. Over the past thirty years, the guiding ideology of "class struggle" has been replaced by concepts of "developing the forces of production", "advanced culture", "the outlook of scientific development", and "harmonious society", but because the latter were all determined by politics and were not part of a philosophy or system of values they lacked the systematic qualities that characterize Western universal values, and this meant that the old political system was always distorted and undermined "ideologically" by the reform of the economic system. As a result, when values float like bubbles that disperse in the air, questions of fragmented reality and artistic questions can all be understood.

In 2010 when I completed *Chinese Art History in the 21st Century: 2000-2010*, in analysing China's contemporary art context since 2000 in the preface of that book, I cited commonplace phenomena in politics, the economy, culture, and society in that decade. In addition, in 2009, in the preface to the English edition of *A History of Art in 20th-Century China*, I cited an April 23 *Financial Times* report and analysis of China's economic development, after which I commented:

My mention of the above news report does not mean that I embrace an offensive, narrow nationalism. What is more, I do not feel that the positive news about China that we see in the daily media in any way justifies a sense of complacency. As a Chinese born in the 1950s, I am well aware that our so-called "upsurge" has come at a great cost, to the point that it would be no exaggeration to say that our current reality faces disastrous problems, such as grave damage to the environment, increased social inequity, and huge disparity in the distribution of wealth.

In fact, people often hear that in different cities and areas problems have reached a most putrid level: the problem of further deterioration of the environment, total corruption (even the claim that there is "universal corruption"), the constant increase in social malignancy, increasingly frequent conflicts between the government and the public, terrorism highlighting ethnic problems, general abuse of power, and a total lack of constraints in the system. In every corner of the Internet there are anxious rumours about dire events. Everything suggests that an "epochal crisis" hangs like a haze over China, a context that conceptual artists interested in intellectual games and artists obsessed with style and taste – the two basic categories of conceptual and narrative art – cannot escape.

Of course, there is always art practice that has differing degrees of relationship with politics and history; what most typically attracts Western attention to the mainland Chinese art scene is the increasingly alienated Ai Weiwei – at least this was the situation prior to Ai Weiwei's August 2015 German media interviews and his exhibition at the Royal Academy of Arts in October that attracted large audiences. Because China's political system has not fundamentally changed in the almost four decades of reform and opening since 1978, most of the time people remain sensitive to art games – whether that involves political engagement or avoidance. In short, artists and critics remain involved with politics.

Artists and critics frequently emphasize that art is art and that it should distance itself from social and political issues. Interestingly, on the one hand, China's centralized system of power generally reminds intellectuals that the space accorded democracy and freedom is very small, and calls for constitutional democracy and universal values constantly appear on Internet media (and in print media if there is ever the opportunity); on the other hand, people in art circles, especially young artists and critics, rarely talk about or discuss such questions. Artists focus internally on extremely individual experiences or even personal sensitivities and vulnerabilities, while critics are keen to pepper their writings with quotations from Gilles Deleuze, Giorgio Agamben, or Jacques Rancière (read in Chinese translation) used in writing articles that avoid describing China's reality, even in a roundabout way. What is complex is that most people realize that simply shouting out slogans about "universal values" has lost any real significance, given that officialdom obviously and tenaciously reminds people to remain on high alert for Western universal values because these concepts from the West have always been considered by officialdom to be a subversion of socialist China. In fact, as Western observers also note: the fragmentation of Iraq, the dark inside stories of the Afghan presidential election, delays in the Iran nuclear negotiations, the dismemberment of the Ukraine and so on expose the failure of Western countries, especially the United States, to promote democratic systems and liberalism – these are after all just one set of theories among many. People question why, if free and democratic political theories and moral truths have basic legitimacy, do we not see effective practices and policies, not to mention actual results? Several years after the Arab colour revolutions seem to have failed, or are only paid lip service, in producing democracies like those of the United States as representative of Western democracy, the actual situation is, in short, a mess. These outcomes of course serve China's rulers well: China should build socialism with its own characteristics, rather than simply copy the Western doctrine of democracy and freedom.

2014 was Xi Jinping's first year in office. He and his team faced a mountain of accumulated problems. His anti-corruption campaign led to fierce resistance from interest groups within the Party that reached the proportions of a Hollywood epic, with the result that people can barely summon up the energy and interest to look at what reform measures have been carried out. At the same time, the issues of military build-up, cyber-espionage, intellectual property rights, and human rights, as well as territorial disputes with Washington's allies, have resulted in increased degrees of tension between China on the one hand and the United States and neighbouring countries on the other, so that at the China-US Strategic and Economic Dialogue in July 2016, Secretary of State John Kerry simply reminded China: building a new strategic relationship between the two countries does not simply rely on language, we need action. In fact, the Dialogue quickly slid from strategic discussions to economic problems, revealing that in Sino-US relations (including China's relations with Western countries), some fundamental issues have not been resolved. Ideological differences remain fundamental, although they are often concealed by language about "national interest". This context goes well beyond the news, but unless a political event is an enjoyable story, Chinese artists and critics pay little attention to this type of news. Most of my circle of friends on WeChat (technological progress, control of opinion, and people's demands have meant that people in China have moved from blogs to direct WeChat) are in the art world, but when I sent them this statement by Kerry, their comments were few compared to the number of comments they make on gossip from within the art world.

Excited by jihadists in the Middle East, Xinjiang separatist groups are committing increasingly violent acts in different cities, so that now there are obvious changes in China's original ideological position in international affairs. Whereas the Chinese Government once supported Arab liberation movements, it now faces threats from ISIS, because this Islamist terrorist organization has announced it will set up

Islamist states throughout the world, including China. For China, the fight against terrorism can obviously become an increasingly regular political and social problem, at the same time as it signifies that the complexity of China's social reality is more global.[3]

In fact, in global politics the consecutive "colour revolutions" of the twenty-first century following the 2003 "rose revolution" in Georgia and the 2010 "jasmine revolution" in Tunisia, and coming in the wake of the revolutions in the late 1980s and early 1990s in Eastern Europe, have seen the rapid spread of a new international political and economic pattern of change to Egypt, Libya, Syria, and Iran, fundamentally changing the face of the Middle East, and this has given rise to the fear that the "colour revolutions" will spread to Asia, especially China. Indeed, as early as 2011, there were rallies in some cities on the Chinese mainland calling for a "jasmine revolution in China", and there has been "a sunflower student movement" in Taiwan, and an "occupy" movement in 2014 in Hong Kong; these were seen by official analysts in China as "colour revolutions" in the Far East that had "mainland China as their ultimate target".[4] The problem is how to understand or interpret these changes in reality, and it is difficult to explain these issues in terms of big power strategy. When Taiwanese students desperately demanded of the authorities that government decisions be open and procedurally fair, the real cause of the outbreak of the "sunflower student movement" becomes apparent.

In any case, the globalization of economies and markets has led to profound changes in different countries in the region, and so-called cultural particularities are an amalgam of particular knowledge within different civilizations. An article in the November 2014 issue of *Die Welt* reported that in 2015, China will have more than 500,000 students studying abroad, which is an amazing figure when compared with previous data.[5] In the author's opinion, even though China has more than seven million college graduates a year, "their knowledge and skills do not meet the needs of modern social and economic development. Studying abroad, one can cultivate the ability to solve problems independently." This means that each generation of Chinese will be more deeply involved in the exchanges and collisions between different civilizations and increasingly more people will be acquiring knowledge that will be increasingly complex and remote from earlier knowledge structures. For China, this will of course mean that Western civilization will be more universal in its influence on young Chinese, and the old political systems of ideological control and political education will also become increasingly ineffective.

Today mainstream ideology is hollowed out as it is increasingly challenged by the ever-developing Internet media. On 1 June 2015, 50 provincial police organizations went online as uniformly identified "police inspections of law enforcement" to focus on Weibo, WeChat and Baidu accounts, which was explained as a measure to prevent "cyber crime" as well as to deter "bad words and deeds online". *Global Times*, addressing those who suspected that this was designed to counter "electronic democracy", provided a vague explanation: "Police have no obligation or responsibility to make moral or political evaluation of any statements on the Internet that do not conflict with the law, and will not pursue those who make legal statements. They are only concerned with those who break the law, particularly serious violators." (*Global Times*, no. 3621, 1 June 2015, p. 14.) *Reference News* (June 1 issue, p. 16) also quoted a BBC online report of May 31: "On May 29, China's Politburo announced that it would set up Communist Party groups in all organizations, including economic, cultural, and social organizations." Anyone with a basic knowledge of Chinese history and society will realize that this is a further measure intended to strengthen, not weaken, the Communist Party's grip on society as a whole, and it is in stark contrast to the reform of the 1980s whereby the Party withdrew from government organizations. Shortly thereafter, *Global Times* ran a story on 29 June 2015 headed "Xiaomi Should Be Applauded by Society for Setting up a Communist Party Committee". The story reported how the Xiaomi Corporation that produces mobile phones held a meeting on 19 June to celebrate the establishment of its Communist Party branch. The company, which has more than 8,000 employees, has 104 Communist Party members. How the company will handle the different values of the Communist Party and the company and to what extent the Communist Party will be able to intervene in the business management process and influence company decisions is unknown to outsiders. But what is certain is that the Party Committee will no doubt have an impact on the operations and management of the company; in addition to the existing Board of Directors, there will be a Communist Party Committee, and in addition to the President and General Manager, there will be a Communist Party Secretary. Regardless of who is to assume the role of Secretary, this clearly recalls the period of the planned economy and it seems similar to the State-owned enterprise management model, unless these new positions are all just empty titles. The newspaper report also explained: "Many private business leaders and executives believe that the average performance of Party members among employees is better than that of non-Party members." The report also demonstrates a skewed logic when it states: "All over the world, large enterprises want to maintain good relations with the ruling party and those who will potentially form a ruling party, and so this is not seen to be a political issue." These baseless analogies and situations are quite staggering, and the report even goes on to say: "China's rapid development in the non-public economy shows that private enterprises perform better when combined with the political system of the country; this is a constructive direction in the long-term development of non-public enterprises" (p. 15).

2015 was an impressive year of market volatility; the "stock market crash", combined with the simultaneous obviously slowing economy and the massive explosion in Tianjin on 12 August, raised serious doubts about China and many people simply said that an era had come to an end. Indeed, the possible ensuing rise in unemployment may have prompted national political strategy to direct people's anxiety and attention towards foreign conflicts which would affect world trade. These were all problems that concerned people. The media seemed to be increasingly saying that the "Chinese economic miracle was coming to an end". This background affected the art market, and of course, regardless of where the funds entering the art market came from, from at least the second half of 2008, starting with the economic crisis, the buoyant contemporary art market was in decline.

Even though slogans proclaiming traditional culture were continually advanced by the Communist Party, by 2015, the Party School of the CPC Central Committee began to systematically introduce central government and local officials to ancient culture, especially Confucianism. When people attempt to interpret the meaning of the "China dream" proposed a few years ago by the party's leader, Xi Jinping, thousands of years of traditional culture are understood to be the cultural gene that will ensure the restoration of Chinese civilization, which will help heal problems caused by the economic slowdown and the stock market collapse. In earlier decades, Party cadres at all levels were primarily required to study and understand Marxism-Leninism and Mao Zedong thought; this requirement has not yet been formally changed, but what is in fact studied is the traditional ideology and moral standards that were criticized from 1949 until 1976, while the Ministry of Education has begun to increase the space devoted to classical literary theory in textbooks. This phenomenon shows that the Communist Party is looking for a reliable and secure system of values, although the present choice does cater to those interested in, or even fascinated by, traditional art. Since the late 1980s "new literati painting" has sailed along smoothly. Around 2014 a "new school of *gongbi* painting" became influential and it met with no official criticism. Some art critics and artists believe that the phenomenon is an ideological and conceptual compromise or a static product. However, even though critics often question the continued use of traditional Chinese painting materials and tools in the face of the use of new materials and ideas, the discussion of "Chinese-style painting" is regarded as something that can only be clarified in the context of the broader issue of Chinese civilization.

People often let issues slide because they are busy or preoccupied and those who run the country and have defined no new spiritual content for the new century were caught off-guard by the announcement of the agreement on 5 October 2015 of the Trans Pacific Partnership, a document setting down the rules for the global economic game for the 21st century led by the United States. China, who had grown complacent with its huge economic development, was reminded: This country splashing its money around had not only lost the power to formulate the rules of the game, but now realizes that it might be too late to try to expedite reforms required by globalization itself as it faces the danger of being abandoned again by the world. Art circles might still see such events as indirect context, but for quite a long time into the future, China's economic problems and the social, political and cultural problems that will also arise, will inevitably affect the art market. In the mid-1990s, Chinese critics began to discuss "getting on the international track" and the related question of international art "standards", and for those critics and related persons trying to obtain the right to assess the value of art, this event again reminds us: will the future art evaluation system come from the West or will it come from a nation that has a long tradition and culture of its own?

Fundamentally speaking, the basis for assessing the value of art is a system of values, and when China in an era of globalization has not yet established a value system that conforms to this era, then it cannot possibly have the power to control or influence art values. On 8 January 2016, the online edition of the *New York Times* reported that a golden statue of Mao Zedong in China had been removed. The paper said that the boss of a rural business had spent the equivalent of $ 465,000 to build the 36-meter-high statue of Mao Zedong and the demolition was ordered by local officials. People who understand recent Chinese history know that no unified evaluation about Mao Zedong and his period of history has ever been reached and this will of course influence China into the future. Officials back in the early 1980s made an evaluation of Mao's record that declared he was seven parts good and three parts bad, although the Central Committee of the Communist Party of China's *Resolution on Some Historical Issues Since the Founding of the Party* (27 June 1981), unequivocally negated Mao's Cultural Revolution, declaring that "practice proved that the 'cultural revolution' was not and could not be any kind of revolution or social progress". Since 1979, the problem of the history and reality of Mao Zedong has emerged as a symbol of different periods. In fact, the thought, political strategy, and system Mao Zedong established, were inextricably linked with the artistic criteria of the past and, whenever required, the fields of culture and art (including their realms of speech and publishing) would invoke those criteria to impose limits and issue political reminders on ideological standards. For example, in 2013 *Beijing Daily* published an article titled "Leave No Space for Universal Values", and the article stated: "Dare to struggle, dare to wield a shining sword. This is our imperative choice!" This readily suggests the tenor of the Cultural Revolution period. However, with the increasing complexity of social and economic life, forms of values and standards become increasingly complex and difficult to demarcate. Art itself has the characteristic of expressing values that are ambiguous and complex, but this official ideology has remained influential and it can be invoked in times of need.

In fact, in the same way as a political and economic "international order" never existed, even though Kissinger, who had a historical relationship with China, has discussed this issue (at the 2015 Beijing International Forum),[6] cultural and artistic standards have never been uniform. There are no artistic criteria, yet art still exists. At a time when more and more Western art exhibitions are held in China, this invariably implies, regardless of the reason, that the influence and power of the art world has changed and shifted. China has become very influential globally because of its economic development, and this impact has challenged the universal stance of adherence to an ideology formed in "hungry Europe". The most typical example is provided by President Xi Jinping's 28 March 2016 visit to the Czech Republic, when "Prague Broke with Precedent in Receiving President Xi" (*Reference News*, 29 March 2016, headline) revealing to the world the changes in European countries: the Czech Republic founded by Havel and the ideological position it maintains has been transformed to allow the national interests of the Czech Republic to accommodate the relationship with the Chinese.[7] Although it is not sure whether the change is irreversible, the Czech Republic's hoped-for Chinese investment "dream" seems to contain ideological considerations.[8] The world is adjusting its historically formed nodes to maintain a balance in accordance with changes in the structural network. China maintains strict limits of ideology, yet in dealing with issues of international relations, it blunts the ideological edge as much as possible, so that sometimes when people watch CCTV's international channel they might think they have switched to a European channel. However, *Global Times* (Tuesday, 29 March 2016, p. 14) stated unabashedly:

China is breaking down the ideological iron curtain in Europe, not by reason, but it is by relying on her economic development that China is attracting attention. For European countries, the benefits of cooperation with China greatly exceed the political benefits of ideological confrontation with China, and this led to a lot of strategic thinking about turning to China.[9]

The 20th century was a century of dramatic changes in a Chinese society mired in misery and, despite the different problems in different periods, art retained its particularity but, to the present day, Chinese art has still not extricated itself from many fundamental issues associated with the past. Today, visitors to the Pace Gallery in Beijing can see photographs by Hiroshi Sugimoto, and students and teachers of the Central Academy of Fine Arts can see works by Jean Baudrillard in the Academy's gallery and can discuss his ideas. Yet Chinese artists and critics still encounter many problems that can be traced back to the early years. This is of course not a bad thing, but this phenomenon reflects the characteristics of Chinese civilization: possibilities for creation exist and endure over time. In fact, art changed and developed from the late-Qing to the China of today with understanding and reflection correlated with that change and development.

Notes

1. In February 2007, Wen Jiabao, as one of the leaders of the Communist Party of China, made the following statement in an article titled "On the Historical Tasks in the Primary Stage of Socialism and Several Problems I Have Encountered in Foreign Policy" (*Guanyu shehui-zhuyi chuji jieduan de lishi renwu he wo guo duiwai zhengce de jige wenti*): "Science, democracy, a legal system, freedom, and human rights are not the exclusive preserve of capitalism, but are values that mankind has pursued in common in the course of a long historical process, and they are the fruits of civilization created together". However, this statement has no bearing on the critique of "universal values". In 2008, Chen Kuiyuan, Head of the Chinese Academy of Social Sciences, made the following criticism: "In the past, Christianity advocated its religious doctrines as universal values, and today the West authoritatively pronounces its 'democratic views', 'views on human rights', and its free market economic theory to be universal values; China is like a shadow following a person when we too talk volubly about wanting to integrate with 'universal values'". Ref: Panorama (*Guangjiaojing*), September-October issue, 2010, no. 456.

2. The main participants in this conference at Ditchley Park (10-12 October 2008) were scholars and professional staff from the British Museum, the Tate, the National Gallery, the Metropolitan Museum in New

York, the San Francisco Museum of Modern Art, Yale University, and Princeton University, together with scholars from France and the Netherlands. Chinese participants included Gao Minglu, Wu Hung, Wang Huangsheng, Zhou Yan, Fei Dawei, Huang Zhuan, Zhu Qi, Wang Jianwei, Zhang Peili, Sui Jianguo, Sheng Rui, and Wang Zhiliang. This conference was convened with the assistance of Lin Mingzhu's China Art Foundation and the English collector Susan Hayden.

3. As a result, at the 2014 APAC meeting in Beijing, China adopted an anti-terror strategy similar to that of other members.

4. *Global Times* reported on 25 November 2014 that the Far Eastern colour revolutions targeted China. The author of the report was Yang Yucai, a professor at the Crisis Management Center of National Defense University.

5. The original article states: "Bis zum Jahr 2009 gingen chinesische Akademiker vorwiegend zu Promotions-, Fortbildungs- oder Forschungsstudien ins Ausland, die meisten davon in die USA. Die jährlichen Zahlen neuer chinesischer Studenten in den Vereinigten Staaten lagen bis zum Jahr 2008 unter 100.000. Heute, fünf Jahre später, sind es dreimal so viele, mehr als 90 Prozent von ihnen sind Selbstzahler. [...] Nach Angaben des Pekinger Erziehungsministeriums

gingen zwischen 1978 und Ende 2013 rund 3,06 Millionen Chinesen zum Auslandsstudium in alle Welt. Darunter waren im Studienjahr 2013 allein 414.000 Schüler und Studenten. Von ihnen entschieden sich mit 236.000 mehr als die Hälfte (beziehungsweise deren Eltern) für US-Eliteschulen und Universitäten. Nach Hochrechnungen für das Kalenderjahr 2014 wird die weltweite Gesamtzahl aller Lernenden aus China auf 460.000 und ab 2015 auf weit mehr als eine halbe Millionen steigen". Based on this data of growth, this second study described middle school students in China as the "quiet revolution". (See *Die Welt*, 24 November 2014).

6. Kissinger said at the Forum: "There has never been a so-called world order, but there must be a world order. Otherwise, we could face the danger of being destroyed." (2 November 2015, the 14th edition of the *Global Times*).

7. This was the first visit to the Czech Republic by a Chinese President since bilateral relations were established. The media commented that over the previous twenty years, President Havel and his centre-right cabinet had focused on the human rights issues in their dealings with Beijing, leading to strained relations.

8. In 2014 the Czech President visiting China told the media that he came to China to "learn how to accel-

erate economic growth and social stability", not "as a professor of the market economy or of human rights".

9. This official newspaper intentionally obscured the widespread anger and dissatisfaction the attitude of the Czech President aroused in his country; many Czech people (especially intellectuals) believed that the presidential position of avoiding human rights and liberal values and simply discussing economic issues was an embarrassment to the Czech Republic. Moreover, they questioned whether economically it would bring real benefits to the Czech people.

Cet ouvrage a été achevé d'imprimer sur les presses de
Graspo (République tchèque) en avril 2018.